A Companionable Way

A Companionable Way

Path of Devotion in Conscious Love

LISA M. HESS

CASCADE *Books* · Eugene, Oregon

A COMPANIONABLE WAY
Path of Devotion in Conscious Love

Copyright © 2016 Lisa M. Hess. All rights reserved. Except for brief quotations in critical publications or reviews, no part of this book may be reproduced in any manner without prior written permission from the publisher. Write: Permissions, Wipf and Stock Publishers, 199 W. 8th Ave., Suite 3, Eugene, OR 97401.

Cascade Books
An Imprint of Wipf and Stock Publishers
199 W. 8th Ave., Suite 3
Eugene, OR 97401

www.wipfandstock.com

PAPERBACK ISBN: 978-1-4982-3736-9
HARDCOVER ISBN: 978-1-4982-3738-3
EBOOK ISBN: 978-1-4982-3737-6

Cataloguing-in-Publication data:

Hess, Lisa M.

A companionable way : path of devotion in conscious love / Lisa M. Hess.

Description: Eugene, OR : Cascade Books, 2016 | Includes bibliographical references.

Identifiers: ISBN 978-1-4982-3736-9 (paperback) | ISBN 978-1-4982-3738-3 (hardcover) | ISBN 978-1-4982-3737-6 (ebook)

Subjects: LSCH: Religions—Relations. | Christianity and other religions. | Dialogue—Religious aspects. | Theology of religions (Christian theology).

Classification: BR127 .H48 2016 (paperback) | BR127 .H48 (ebook)

Manufactured in the U.S.A.   09/15/16

Dedicated to
the motherline I can name,
seven generations are we:
Martha Engle, Elizabeth Brenner,
Catherine Newcomer, Elizabeth N. Musser,
Ruth Berger, Carol Virginia—

and

Mary Pierce Brosmer,
whose vision, passion, and willing woundedness
have restored so many of us.

Contents

Preface (How to Read this Book) | ix
Acknowledgments | xiii

In Search of . . . | 1
Introduction | 2
Grounding in Exile | 20
Desire | 25
Deep Roots in Difference | 33
Liturgical Hospitality | 38
Belief amidst Nontheism and Other | 46
Path of Conscious Love | 51
Fidelity in the Fear of Betrayal | 65
Devotion | 70
Befriending Outsiders | 78
Seeing With the Heart | 83
Rebirthing | 93
Awakening | 97
Deepening—Into the Dark of Initiation | 103
A New-Old Sacred | 107
Circle | 115
Conclusion | 133

Bibliography | 139

Preface (How to Read this Book)

This is a book for conscious loving in divisive times, which means it cannot be read from start to finish, nor should it be read quickly. It invites you into a spiraling journey of holy desire and sacred work, therefore in the nonlinear, episodic fashion you determine. This is an adventure only you can choose, then choose to stay with when its demands confront you. You may uncover your deepest Self, your own deepest wisdom within the Wisdom of ages crafted specifically within you. I found the way here when I became responsible for developing a master's level course on "interreligious and intercultural encounter," which ultimately offered fruit I had neither anticipated nor sought. From here emerges good work worth doing in a world hungry for it. Healthy relationships seed and blossom here with others whose lives also open to unexpected invitation. I have Christian language for this, as that is my home tradition, but these pages emerge from significant encounters with strangers and spirit-friends in other historic traditions and no tradition at all. Conscious loving in divisive times requires a disruptive, potentially peaceable awakening in each of us toward the blessed assurance that comes when living into rigorous abundance able to hold the suffering of self and others.

A Companionable Way resisted straightforward prose for nearly four years before becoming this collection of stories and reflections, experienced with spirit-friends across differences of many kinds. As a theological scholar, I had attempted to place this unfolding journey of devotion into the academic learning/teaching genre. There I would state the problem and survey the field, honoring the resources received to address the problem and even solve it. I would have woven the voices together in a tight, analytical argument to persuade your mind and heart of the significance of the problem *and* the innovation of the solution. I became full professor in a freestanding Christian seminary by doing just that kind of work. Then I

Preface (How to Read this Book)

read Judith Duerk's *Circle of Stones*, an invitational, interactive, and intuitive book exploring *inner/outer transformation* in a *nonlinear, even spiraling journey fashion*. As obvious as it may be to some of us, my theology-professor heart finally *got it*, at least for this work. *Inviting* an *interactive, intuitive* journey into devotion in conscious love requires *invitational, intuitive,* and *interactive language*, be it poetry, prose, or somewhere in between. My years-long struggle was with genre more than content, *how* to share with integrity what I have received more than *what* the words might be.

True to our divisive times, you have a decision to make in how you proceed. If you identify within a historic wisdom tradition, particularly an institutionally mainline and/or more hierarchical or intellectually expressed Western/European one (those strands of Protestant or Catholic Christianity, Mormon, secularist, etc.), then I invite you to read slowly, but as traditional custom dictates: from the front to the back, linear order. An introduction outlines the conceptual intentions of the work, and you can begin to listen to your own voice and experience amidst the "yearnings" and "habits of minds" that drive and divide our world into many worlds, often at odds with one another. You can decide whether you want to focus on the more interpretive chapters or whether you have the patience to enter into various stories of encounter for what might arise in you in more inarticulate or intuitive response, underneath or before the interpretive language offered.

If you are more a seeker, by which I mean you find your center and energies grounded in a more fluid, nonlinear, secular feel of equanimity, then I invite you to begin with the last chapter, "Circle." With that as foundation, you may then receive the encounter stories, refrains, and interpretive writings in a fashion well suited to your own proclivities and habits of mind. Your gift has already been finding grounding "out there," bringing it to the wholes in your life from the ground "up." You might read the sections in reverse order, from "Circle" back toward the table of contents, or choose whatever order attracts you. In either case, the text offers you choice in how to best receive what is offered in good will, with open-hearted intention. A nonlinear journey needs to be open from multiple vantage points, so this text lives into that reality.

What I am attempting to share beckons from opposite directions, after all—establishment and "out there," tradition and no tradition at all—as well as the numerous places "in between." No matter how you self-identify, we may all meet metaphorically and energetically in the central teaching of the

PREFACE (HOW TO READ THIS BOOK)

book, which is *devotion*. Devotion is the word that found me for the embodied receiving/awakening to the Holy that unifies without power, loves without attachment, opens without expectation of return. At least as much as each of us can withstand the Holy, its river of devotion, and the invitation to practice this in body. Devotion is the single-point flow out of which unity and interdependence can actually be *sensed* and *seen*. Devotion lives within an embodied heart more than intellect as conceived today. From this place, all discourse about *encounter*, about interreligious-intercultural learning, begins in earnest toward peaceable awakening and an expressive delight able to companion the suffering of self and other.

Academically inclined readers may find the text imbalanced and repetitive as it spirals through similar or related themes from several different directions. In the mental habits of what Walter Ong calls "the literate mind,"[1] *A Companionable Way* may even be deemed uncritical, with an overreliance upon personal experience to suggest future directions of engaged scholarship. I no longer accept that judgment as determinative for what needs saying. We teach and learn best when we share precisely where we are without the smoke and mirrors of abstraction and obfuscation. Our captivity in fear and violence require new risks and willingness to be seen. Duerk's work taught me me to invite you into this journey with much more transparency.

Actual encounters and stories offer you a narrative feel of some of the terrain that welcomes and divides us today, whether religious, political, or cultural. A refrain accompanies each section, which you are encouraged to ponder, digest, sense your way into, feel what rises. The final portion of each section then gives a more textual interpretation of the themes needed to keep my own balance in a journey of devotion in conscious love. I offer here some of the most psychologically and spiritually demanding material I know, which makes repetition and engagement from several angles absolutely necessary.

A Companionable Way therefore offers you a *both/and* of expertise and invitation. While I suspect the expertise acquired will only be minimally useful to you, I am well credentialed and established in both mainline and seeker/nonhierarchical communities. I have worked hard to get where I am, taking pleasure in it. Still, the outward work dims greatly in light of the inner work required to write here. The intention is to offer whatever of this journey will feed your own bodysoul and to encourage you to relinquish all

---

1. Ong, *Orality and Literacy*, 100–102.

else without thought, reliant upon your own embodied wisdom. I hear Walt Whitman smiling as he sings in our ears, "Re-examine all you have been told at school or church or in any book, dismiss whatever insults your own soul, and your very flesh shall be a great poem and have the richest fluency not only in its words but in the silent lines of its lips and face and between the lashes of your eyes and in every motion and joint of your body."[2] Amen to that, which is the gift I had to learn to give myself in order to arrive here, sharing this invitation with you.

All rests within the image of a "circle of stones," an ancient-new space of stones *and* the necessary spaces between them. I offer you hard-won words *and* the necessary silences out of which they emerged. You are welcome to the contributions of my journey, but for it to matter, you must learn to name your own experience, accountability, and yearnings as they arise in you—a process less and less traditioned in our fearfully bound schooling. The transfiguration of each of us, individuals immersed in community, whether we desire it or not, requires this both/and genre of prose made flesh. The more deeply listening, widely devoted, consciously loving and heart-seeing human beings there are in the world, the better and safer it will be for all of us.

---

2. Whitman, preface to *Leaves of Grass*, 11.

Acknowledgments

So many hearts have shaped this work, which is now offered outwardly in hopes of honoring and protecting these hearts in the One who called us into companionship. Writing about the transfigurative force of spiritual companionship presents a fascinating conundrum. How do you proclaim the best news and abundance of sacred human belonging you have ever known while protecting the intimacies of soul and learning that were for you alone, both of you, each of you? How do you describe the pattern and power of companionship in an abundance that just cannot be contained while disguising enough detail so that the vulnerabilities risked and shared remain private, protected? These pages are my best attempt to do just that: to be faithful to what we were given, so to share what I learned from each of you, which *is* needed in our polarized and polarizing world today, overflowing with yearnings and habits of mind not as well met as they might be. What follows here is *true* to my experience AND where necessary, details have been changed to honor those who risked so much to help me learn, to see and hear me into what I now know.

One Thursday, September 11th of 2008, I began a teaching collaboration with a rabbinic companion willing to make the journeys to teach and learn together in a seminary classroom. His willingness to pursue wisdom across traditions and in unexpected venues transformed my life. My own awakening, my own focus, expanded and deepened in ways neither of us knew would happen. I found myself welcomed into webs of tradition and spiritual practices in far-flung corners of the United States, from my own home in the Midwest. These pages emerge from companionships with men and women in California, Nebraska, New York, Texas, Massachusetts, Florida, and various locations in between. This year, on this same significant date, I am surprised and smiling to complete the work that has nested and hibernated from so long ago until now. I bow with deep gratitude to

Acknowledgments

all those at Wipf and Stock/Cascade Books, specifically Charlie Collier and Jacob Martin, for their commitment, publishing model, and faithful willingness to take risks on nontraditional publishing projects. You give authors courage and the world innovation. Thank you.

None of it would have found this form, but for Women Writing for (a) Change, a non-traditional writing school for women and men founded by Mary Pierce Brosmer twenty-five years ago in Cincinnati, Ohio. As a HearthKeeper (which means a graduate of the 2013 Conscious Feminine Leadership Academy) and a regular Wednesday Night writer, I came to voice in countless small groups, and large-group and public readarounds. Women holding space for women to come to words—nameless and unseen work, often, but fundamental to everything that follows here. I wish I could name you all by name *and* I want to honor the intimacy of our circles. Details about the community, now with affiliate sites across the country, may be found at www.womenwriting.org.

Spirit sent me two tenaciously faithful ones I need to thank by name, as the Trinitarian dance of the three of us has birthed this work. Lisa Dawn Michael Heckaman, close friend and companion in the sacred work that calls us both forward—the work of healing in womanheart-spaces held for both men and women—and Brian Daniel Maguire—husband and friend who has wrestled and grown alongside me as the life of deep feeling overtook us, a choiceless choice we both continue to honor in one another. The willingness and remarkable tenacity in each of you to companion me in this creative endeavor continue to bless me. *Thank you.* May all our efforts offer merit forward to any and all who yearn for what we have learned together in the One who calls us forth, day after day.

Lisa M. Hess
September 11, 2015

In Search of . . .

a peaceable way of awakening, becoming uniquely human across irreconcilable difference
sacred heart, abundant devotion, undying compassion, pure awareness
God, Goddess, Mother, Father, Son, Spirit, Divine, Holy, Wisdom, YHWH, and more names than can be counted—each distinct, all without division, separation, changeability, mixture
that which has no name at all
an expressive delight, able to companion suffering of self and others

Some time ago, many years into a future only envisioned, in many places on earth, a search took root in the hearts, minds, and bodies of creation. It came to words in human beings fearfully mired in learned hatreds . . . human beings unknowingly beckoned by a deeper way of healing, within and beyond themselves. The search was borne by all the world, seen and unseen. Drawn forward by that which was sought, a way of companionship began, inviting a return to the body, a path of devotion in conscious love across difference, a trusting in the quiet holy dark forgotten in fear. In that living, breathing center, many now await, listening, beginning to learn what will nourish and heal.

Introduction

I was running sacred, though I felt only scarred and scared. A young doctoral student in theology and a budding religious leader within a local church in New Jersey, I faced challenges that overwhelmed and rising emotional energies that unnerved me. The retreat center close to where I lived offered a good running trail, complete with paved and beachfront trails. I was running more, and longer, almost as if I were afraid of something behind me, within me. Whatever it was, it was so close I could not seem to get away. The more deeply I felt it, the longer and faster I ran, not unlike a horse increasingly frightened by a driverless wagon hitched behind her. I entered a grotto near the end of a looped run, dappled by sun and shade. A Marian figurine towered above, whitened by the sun but for dark specks where it had been weathered. Two faded turquoise kneelers rested at the grotto's base. Without anymore straightaways to run, I slowed to a canter, then to a trot, then to a walk. Exhausted, I lowered my body onto the faded pads of a kneeler. It felt strange to me, a running Protestant reined in close to a blessed Mother.

I looked up at her, of professed blessed status unknown to me. I heard myself ask what it was like for her: *What was it like in your body of inconceivably sacred purpose?* A question of sacred trajectory, when I thought about it later. Tradition has it Mary sang praises in response: *My soul magnifies the Lord, and my spirit rejoices in God my savior.* She speaks to her soul enlargening, *making visible*, the Lord. Of course, other words come with such churched ears: *This is my body, given for you.* These words bring intimations of sacramental bread, wine or juice, a solemnity formalized in the hands of men (mostly), though some women now. Myself included there. Years later, I would learn the archaeological and archetypal significance of grottos for the Feminine. I would begin to see Marianist grottos are a Christianized integration of rituals and symbols centuries old in records of the Moon

Introduction

Goddess, represented in numerous civilizations both East and West.[1] But back then, I was not ready to know that.

When I was running from something I knew not, I stopped finally in a Marianist grotto. I could not outrun what was rising from so deep within me, nor was I willing any longer to try. Unknowing, I was entering into an internal-external transfiguration that would be a *return to the body* as sacred word and an invitation into deep feeling that is redemptive, illuminating, integrative. I was finding my way into a *path of devotion in conscious love* known in ancient-new sacred belonging: spiritual companionships and circle-way wisdom. Ultimately, Marianist grottos became the places in my life that "could hold me" as a holy enfleshed woman awakening to deep feeling on a path of devotion in conscious love. A contemplative path unfolded, rooting itself deeply in the body and in multiple, spiritual friendships across irreconcilable difference.

This path of devotion has been more nourishing and challenging than any one community of practice in which I belong, largely because it overflowed the bounds of my sense of "community of practice," beyond my understandings of congregation, faith, religion, and tradition. I found myself guided into a holy meander in spiritual friendships with practitioners of various traditions, or no identifiable tradition at all. Many of us relied heavily upon our root communities—congregations steeped in textual traditions or local sanghas of lineages of practice. Others challenged such "communities," finding connection, intimacy, and transformation completely outside of them. This unexpectedly transformed the habits of mind I had had about my own tradition, what belonging means. Even as a clergywoman and a theology professor, I was pushed outside of thinking in these terms at all.

A glimpse of the stories to come, then. Shortly after my run at the New Jersey retreat center, a woman sitting with me on the bench there touched my hand in a commitment of spiritual friendship, which over time released decades of embroiled body-shame in a gentle, bounded, but visceral way. Years later, I as a professor and preacher's wife was manhandled by an unthinking fellow during a congregational coffee hour. It took nearly five years for the theological reality of reconciliation to emerge, but when it did, I knew it deeply in my bones. Invited by a new friend, I found myself face to face with a large Buddha, welcomed over years to learn a felt sense of lovingkindness in (for me) a most unusual fashion. At another grotto close

---

1. Harding, *Woman's Mysteries*, 128.

to my home, a rabbi blessed me with a Passover question, an invitation to release "some inner betrayal" that had captivated me. I knew not what he meant, but posted the intention to release it at an interfaith campus seder. Life opened a couple weeks later, healing the longstanding splinter that the manhandling was in my own body. Doors opened amidst my seminary teaching, then, to a visit in the Bronx where I both "stormed a shtiebel" after sitting with storage and found myself woven into spiritual friendship deeper than a really difficult encounter there. A couple years before that, my husband and I found ourselves at a Shabbat table with a Chabad rabbi and his wife, all of us filled to overflowing. Much later, on a completely inarticulate and intuitive impulse, I drove more than five hundred miles to leave a pomegranate on the gravestone of my great-grandmother. Shortly after that, a New Moon circle of wilding and wizened women gathered to listen deeply to their lives, to name intentions for the coming month. I as theology professor found myself reborn in an unexpected way. Only a few, there are so many others . . .

A Companionable Way shares these stories and the sense I make of them for living a life of deepening sacred purpose in a divisive world. It invites anyone willing into compassionate companionship toward an expressive delight in which all may hold the suffering of self and others. It addresses the deeply human yearning that draws us together and the divisive habits of mind that drive us apart—both movements necessary for inner and outer transformation. It invites you to practice trusting into new flows of befriending, to immerse yourself in the invited and long-held wisdom of others while you listen to your own embodied voices. To do so, this companionable way opens into a path of devotion—a deeply embodied, bounded, and driving force that both purifies and transforms us from the inside out. All this has led to and now requires a new-old "container"—a shape of human gathering—better able to receive and honor all that the world pours into us today: a circle. A companionable way is ultimately a circle way of living into the world. To *think* your way there, consider the yearnings and habits of mind in which we live today.

YEARNING

Within each communal gathering where I am welcomed, whether it takes place within a certain tradition or no tradition, I sense how increasingly hungry each of us is for . . . something. This yearning drives each of us,

INTRODUCTION

albeit in different directions: some of us outward, others of us inward, even more of us into a numbness or distraction of some kind. For me, I name this a hunger to be seen, to be heard, simply to be enough *just as I am*—whether "I" be woman, man, child, elder. Call it a basic human need, right up there with food, shelter, and clothing. Or the relational "seed" so necessary to counterbalance an individualism that isolates. More and more of us are sensing these yearnings,[2] naming them as variously as our stories lead.

So much in our world shapes us to evade and minimize them, however. The *ways* in which we are seen, heard, and expected to perform (conform?) today are increasingly fraught with fear, innuendo, and disconnection. Most collective gatherings can become unexpected minefields of presumption, prejudice, and ideology where we need to hide basic parts of ourselves. In very real ways, it *is* dangerous today to be deeply seen in our human frailty and giftedness. Public condemnation is quick and intense, if perhaps fleeting, before it lands on another unsuspecting and unfortunate soul in undesired trials. Presumption of guilt is fueled by whatever projected fears govern the moment. Think of the most recent scandal, the foibled politician, the immoral religious leader, the abusive athlete, the sexualized teenage celebrity being prepared for cultural consumption. How quickly we are moved to an unconscious fear or anxiety about *what if*. How quickly we move—or are moved—to judge and disassociate. Being deeply seen and heard today carries risks of misunderstanding, abuse, even accusation within a polarized public.

At elemental levels, therefore, we go unseen, unheard, yearning to connect while being saddled with a decreasing awareness in *how*. Without formation and practice, we know less and less about *how* to connect deeply with one another. Our previous ways of gathering—as well as the amount of time we remain in one place—do not allow consistent skill development or the emotional formation for how to connect with one another. Without heightening awareness of it, we are "taught" every day to *disconnect* and rarely how to *connect*. The yearning grows. The urgency is leading to violence in many of us.

Few institutions today are structured well to meet this yearning. The naysayers of our world point to the crumbling institutions, the horrific state of human relations across race, nationality, gender, orientation, political party, and more. Listening to the news, it's hard not to be overwhelmed by hopelessness. Many historic religious traditions are declining

2. Kula and Loewenthal, *Yearnings*, 129–82.

in membership. Government is polarized and fraught. Marriage is changing, and families increasingly take diverse forms today. This grieves some of us terribly and welcomes all of us uncertainly. From the other direction, the visionaries, the idealist ones, paint pictures for us in their words and websites about the magic that is all around, the power of positive listening, the creative life that is at our fingertips if we just . . . (fill in the blank). Somewhere in the middle, each of us receives the perhaps undesired but unavoidable challenge of making a life in a complicated time rife with overwhelming choice. *How then shall we live?* ask the poet-authors Wayne Muller and Terry Tempest Williams. *What do you want to do with your one wild and precious life?* asks another, Mary Oliver.

These pages invite you into recent and tentative answers to such questions, facing yearnings well met and new habits of mind able to hold more than our current divisions. On this path of devotion in conscious love, I was awakened to see and be seen in a fashion beyond my own tradition, though deeply faithful within it. In circle-way communities, I have been heard more deeply than I ever knew possible. As a theology professor and Presbyterian clergywoman, I am a deeply traditioned woman, yet I was given myself anew—found myself reborn—when I became grounded in exile as a befriended outsider, when I sat at table with spirit-friends across irreconcilable difference, when I found myself a theist at home in non- or no-theisms, when I was welcomed in a circle of wilding women. As such, *A Companionable Way* is a record of my own spiritual adventure to companion anyone awakening to a nameless, potentially fearful yearning that was previously unknown, even a little unwelcome. That sneaking suspicion that life was meant to hold more than it seems to? Or this curiosity to trust God more than you ever knew possible, even when all the voices in your head tell you it is dangerous to do so? I welcome you to breathe into this "more" both within the institutions that hold your life and in a wondrous life unfolding "outside" of them. Perhaps these categories of "tradition or not" no longer serve us or name the search as well as they have before. Which means our *habits of mind* must also be redressed.

HABITS OF MIND

A young woman startles awake, finding herself driving an 18-wheeler. She watches herself driving safely, soundly, but cannot recall how she got there. She has no recollection of training to drive a semi, but

Introduction

this is precisely what she seems to be doing. Without much thought, she drives through tree-lined streets of rather bland, suburban, North American neighborhoods. On the passenger's seat beside her lies a map that she has followed step by step. Finally, she turns right into a cobblestone driveway. After the long winding drive, she pulls up in front of an old colonial mansion, bright red brick, white trim. She observes with pleasure its spacious lawns, flowing down a steep decline off to the side of the truck. Behind her is the labyrinthine driveway, lined with ancient elm trees and dappled sunlight. In the distance beyond the lawn lies well-trimmed landscaping, bountiful beds of multicolored flowers. With the semi slowing into the driveway, the cab turns at a right angle to the trailer, grinding the goods to a halt. The engine stalls. With some alarm, she realizes she cannot move forward or backward. There is no way to drive a semi down the slope without great harm to her, the semi, and the goods in the trailer. She cannot move backward, with the trailer of such size and the angle of the cab and driveway. Anger and curiosity begin to arise in her as she wonders whether the map was misleading. "I have been betrayed," she says, to no one in particular. She opens the door, jumps down from the cab, opens the back of the truck and starts unloading the boxes, one by one.

These reflections demonstrate one way to unload our conceptual boxes: boxes of our minds, whether steeped in a tradition or not, to look anew for what can speak peaceably today; boxes of how we live our lives, looking for old-new ways in which more of us may find deeper human being; and boxes of the ways we have been conditioned to think about who we are in community or how community needs to be. The dream above arrived several years ago, spurring me to ask much more radical (at the root) questions than my professional degrees, ecclesial ordination (Presbyterian Church USA), or successful establishment life would ever directly encourage. In what "communities" or "containers" do you spend your time—religious, civic, political, familial? Are you willing to reflect critically on this, perhaps see some things you'd rather not see? Most of us do our best to live within the streams of human belonging we've been given, afraid it will be "worse" on "the outside." To become critically reflective about "our tribe" can threaten the ground on which we live our lives.

For instance, a dear friend found herself in a fundamentalist religious community close to home, yearning for the community while trying to quiet the dissonant voices. She disagreed with the cognitive norms of doctrinal exclusivity and internal conformity required to belong there, but she had also learned to hold her nose and tolerate it for the sake of belonging. As she found herself in a more egalitarian community that fed her spirit "on the outside," she began to "unpack her own boxes." She began to ask questions and gently open her heart to others in new ways. She then discovered herself perceived as a threat in her faith community. High exclusion, after all. Or consider politics. My uncle found his sense of belonging in grassroots politics. Organizing campaigns guided him to deeper connection with others, at least until the campaign was over. Then his community would unravel and he would have to start all over again. Itinerant communities of temporal purpose. In these instances, and perhaps more of your own, communities of practice defined by religious tradition, political persuasion, or other named-identity groups are less and less able to cultivate the deeply embodied habits of mind needed to reconcile the tensions we face.

A Companionable Way therefore opens boxes and allows each of us to examine their contents in some surprising ways—steady, slow, curious. It suggests that the conceptual categories or "habits of mind" so prevalent today are simply no longer the best way to move the goods of heart into a world of wonder and need. Talking, deepening the discourse, argument and counterargument have had their time in the spotlight but now must bow to other ways of engagement. The ways we "see the obvious" need to open anew in different ways of being together that are rooted in invitation, not obligation, and that presume good will, even in the face of violence and betrayal. Our mental habits need to be held more loosely in a love that liberates (thank you, Maya Angelou), all while resisting the immediate critique and judgment of expert rationalists promising the certainty we crave. *You don't have to believe everything you think*—a good bumper sticker I saw once. Sometimes allowing thoughts that discomfort you is the way toward a deeper love and life than your mind could ever hold. Contemplative practice, new flows of spiritual friendship, and strong "containers" able to hold deep feelings—from intense joy to righteous rage without social cost—will invite us into embodied, nondualistic habits of mind, sustained in a simple but spiritually demanding fashion beyond polarized-polarizing identities.

Having been invited for years on this journey, I am now inviting any with ears to hear: unload your own boxes; examine the contents of your life through the inner work of your mind-body-spirit. Learn to place only the necessary nourishment and simplest tools you find into a knapsack to carry on the road with those you will meet on the way. It will take some time to walk past the trucks of certainty, the sculpted gardens, and the colonial

Introduction

architecture of how we've crafted our worlds before. A different kind of journey into unshakable abundance and assurance beckons all of us who are willing.

WHAT *A COMPANIONABLE WAY* IS NOT

Perhaps a glimpse into what this book *is not* will help make it more comprehensible in the words we do have. This is not a book on interfaith dialogue or world religions. *A Companionable Way*, as intended here, offers stories, a rhythmic framework, and some commentary on practices suitable for deepening interpersonal encounters across differences of all kinds. It's not "interfaith dialogue" as traditionally conceived, though those efforts have borne much fruit in what arises here. Dialogue, in the popular mind at least, prioritizes expertise and language, no matter how attentive we may try to be to relationships first, heart-connection first. Focusing on themes or issues may aid understanding, but those also may distract from *sensing* the incontrovertible sacred in an "other" you are trying to understand, at some distance from yourself. It almost presupposes that for fidelity's sake, you will choose your "tradition" over another human being, over another *life*. The dialectics of discourse require either/or choices at almost every turn. A companionable way is more interested in the wordless, the implicit, the structural, the choiceless choices of the numinous become present, the claims on your life interconnected with others in the face of conceived and perceived traditions.

Also in some contrast, discourses on "world religions" presume an abstraction between doing and being, person and practice, which is a conceptual device useful for its purposes, as far as they go. The split is not useful here, however. Learning *about* a religion, even when facts and holidays and histories are intellectually conceived, keeps you at some distance from yourself, from an "other." Companionship is not "learning about" but "learning with." "World religions" feels a bit like the old-school museum, with dead things pinned to velvet cushions for voyeurs to gaze upon, in abstraction and isolation. At best, we come away with the presumption that "they" (Islam, say, as some "force out there") or "we" know something, without ever having to encounter ourselves already in relation, which we are—energetically, spiritually, emotionally—whether we want to be awake to it or not.

A Companionable Way

A companionable way is a stumbling attempt to live first from interdependence amidst irreconcilable difference, to see with the heart first from connection and presumed good will. *Stumbling* may be the most important word there, because there is no way to "get this right" or encounter without "mistakes." Beginning with interdependence requires difficult inner work to encounter our own deeply embodied traditions or habits of mind, laden in the subconscious and unconscious, shaping everything we perceive about something "out there." This inner work is important because without it we may become inoculated against even a remote curiosity about centuries-long wisdom traditions from all over the globe—traditions that could contribute to global healing and relief of suffering, were they encountered in a more suitable fashion of exploration, humility, and discovery. At best, *with* the presumed good will and intention for inner work, living from interdependence becomes a practice, which may allow us to discover ourselves becoming more deeply devoted to others we've just met, strangers become companions.

Lastly, while I am a scholar within a particular academic discipline, the form of my reflections here will not be one of traditional, analytical argument within my discipline. Because primarily relational learning begins and ends in *deep feeling*, the traditional scholarly resources and genre of discourse available today are simply inadequate to my purpose. I think it's fair to say most scholars do not appear to be the most emotionally savvy of us all. We can be the worst offenders of projection and transference. We may actually get socially penalized in our profession for overt emotional displays, except perhaps cognitive aggression. So we devote our lives to increasingly refined points of textual inquiry—what some have joked about as "learning more and more about less and less." We may be driven by something deep within us, often incomprehensible to others, sometimes inaccessible even to us. Instead of delving within, we focus our work beyond—which can be useful, of course . . . until it's not. Myself, I have found the rising awareness about—and in—*deep feeling* to be one of the most destabilizing learnings in my decades of scholarship. Better to pour that drive outside into rigorous scholarship than face it within, I thought. But then . . .

I was found and welcomed into an ancient-new, strong "container" in which to see and be seen, listen and be heard underneath and beyond all my words: a circle. Circle-way communities of practice, new configurations of power and speech, practices of psychological holding and being held while the deeper inner work of self-transfiguration happened . . . "Love"

Introduction

blossomed in ways and with companions it wasn't expected or anticipated to be. "Church" happened within and then beyond traditional church walls, in communities of practice and holy intention. "Body" became a site of revelation, knowledge, and wisdom trumping all professions of gospel and law. "Knowledge" grew from seeds and in dimensions previously suspect and considered insignificant. "Family" expanded beyond bloodlines, with predictable backlash from blood-family. And "God" blew out of every box previously conceived or about to be conceived. And what was the ancient-new, strong container in each of these companionships, the holding spaces in which each attends to his/her own inner work and all co-create the sacred space within which to listen, lament, celebrate, and heal self and world? A *circle space*, womblike and holding, practiced and deepened by both women and men in holy intention. The final chapter of this text lands on precisely what this means and how the form holds all it does.

A COMPANIONABLE WAY EMERGES . . .

This *is* an invitation arising from both the privilege of establishment and the painful gifts of exile. Its pathway to abundance and assurance within me emerged from a stable early family life, steeped in congregational Presbyterian Christianity. Hard work and good fortune have offered me a successful professional life, begun in the liberal arts before being drawn into "higher" theological education, and a blessed marriage to a handsome and tenaciously loyal man. Of course, he is now inevitably torn, perhaps even irretrievably, between his own sacred calling to "his church" and companioning the obstreperous, no less sacred calling of his wife whose "faith community" overflows our one, shared root-tradition. Dear souls . . . This unwieldy life continually disrupts certainties, which is understandably difficult.

Imagine our mutual surprise when the first year of his congregational calling ejected me into exile, a nameless space outside of our previously shared, sacred work. I landed again and again in spaces not immediately or obviously assured of sacred intention, at least as we had been trained to conceive of it. Over months, then years, I landed and grew to trust this Holy more and more deeply in a web of companionships of practice and observance, including Tibetan Buddhists, Jews of Conservative, Modern Orthodox, and Hasidic hue, practitioners of earth-centered spirituality (and those faithful to One they call Goddess), atheists, "nones," and more.

Without expectation or conscious intention for it, in these ways and spaces, persons and places, I discovered a depth of devotion to Jesus as Risen Lord as I traveled with and was nourished by those outside my tradition. The felt sense of this Jesus in the power of the Spirit still overwhelms me today. The felt sense and multiple-tradition receivings of it, however, mean mono-traditional language could never adequately describe it. Solely Christian-communal terms are simply insufficient. In an odd, counterintuitive conviction, I grew to trust Jesus so thoroughly to show up "on the other side" that I learned "He" was always there, the Christ-within Who needs no name within wordless devotion.

So what is a woman of faith to do when she senses the sacred, the Holy One, outside of her community's "boxes," more often outside her community of faith where she is Led than within its previous bounds or language? *Leave church*?[3] Contrary to any expectation of leaving, all this led to *unexpected leadership*—elected roles in church and liturgical-curricular leadership in seminary and guild contexts of higher theological education. As each invitation to lead arrived, I discerned them with my multiply-traditional "community of faith," which had fewer Christians in it by that time. All of us knew leadership was the path to share what I was learning from the peripheries, at the intersections, back into "the center" of my own Christian communion. I accepted the invitations, confirmed mostly by "outsiders." Still, all along, a sense of dissonance grew—fears of disloyalty, even betrayal—right alongside incontrovertible fruit of Spirit and blessed assurance.

The Fidelity in Fear of Betrayal

Peter Rollins coined an important phrase for me in these years: *the fidelity of betrayal*.[4] He delves into the complicated traditions swirling around Judas Iscariot, observing that salvation history within Christian traditions pivots upon Judas's perceived-real betrayal of Jesus in the garden. This incontrovertible both/and would disconcert most Christians today, of course: Judas as necessary to salvation? Judas as faithful disciple with a difficult task? For so very many, *faith* can only mean an unshakable grasping of Jesus's name, work, power, focused on certainties of light as previously conceived, named

---

3. Thankful nod to Barbara Brown Taylor, whose *Leaving Church* was an important text for me at that time.

4. Rollins, *Fidelity of Betrayal*, 13.

Introduction

of old. Yet my own experience and the felt sense in my body convict me in a faith strengthened, deepened, broadened—so much so that I can now withstand in breathing compassion those who judge me falsely, condemn me without question, disregard me and my feelings in public and private ways. This blessed assurance and love from abundance has allowed me to move into the world with more risked compassion than I have ever known. Does my willingness to move into the fear of betrayal, even into a perceived betrayal "outside" of my own community's norms, demonstrate less faith ... or *more*?

Recently, I noticed that only one voice spoke in the dream above. "I have been betrayed," it said. The map the dream-driver was given was somehow "misleading." I began to look for when the word *betrayal* arose these last years. In the grotto, an important yet still inarticulate healing happened when I was invited to release an "inner betrayal" I knew not how to conceive. Leaning into that, even not knowing what it was, led to theological reconciliation and new insight, new connections in companionship. Whatever else this journey entailed, a theme of fidelity and betrayal appears to weave throughout it.

Betrayal is an ugly word, and certainly not one I thought I'd use early on in a book on devotion as the path of conscious love. I have avoided and softened the word for years now, so discomfited have I been with the possibility of betraying myself, my faith, my life in this pathway of relationship. What I have learned is that betrayal can be a doorway to deepened faith, when healed in the sacred gaze of devotion and held in old-new containers strong enough to honor both the light *and holy dark* of human lives. On its own, without conscious care, betrayal destroys, disassembles, and divides. With conscious care, deep-body listening, and willingness to risk, however, the perceived (or real) betrayals of my community of faith have led to deepened faith in me, multiple intimate spiritual companionships, greater self- and other-compassion in an intensely grounded life of assurance and devotion, able to hold the suffering of self and others. In Christian traditions, we call that *fruit of Spirit*.

Standing on this side of my life's calling, knowing my own wholeness more than I ever knew possible, I can concur with the dream-driver's statement: *I have been betrayed* . . . by centuries of yearnings unmet and habits of mind unwilling to expand to the More that awaits us all. Speaking as a *woman* of faith, I find it loyal to betray institutions that have undervalued and dehumanized women for centuries. My sense of loyalty-faith-passion *demanded* a betrayal, perceived or real. After all, when is growth beyond the bounds of *what was* a betrayal, and when is it necessary for healing, for wholeness? I'm beginning to sense that betrayal is inevitable in human life. Each of us *will* be betrayed—by another, by ourselves, by the customs and institutions we hold most dear. We will be exposed to danger by giving information to a (perceived) enemy. Knowledge will be offered, dispersed, that is treacherous to what we hold most dear—our planet, our relationships, ourselves. And sometimes, in the face of deep suffering and hunger, disloyalty is more virtuous than loyalty. Betrayal can be a pathway to deeper fidelity.

Yet it is also true that I have not been betrayed *by anyone in particular*. Not my family, nor my husband, nor my faith community, nor my colleagues. It has taken me decades to be able to name my own experience, especially as it threatens many of those I love—a gentle father and ever-present mother, an attentive husband, a remarkable extended family and faithful web of colleagues and friends. The dream above arrived several years ago, startling me as a Presbyterian, patristic, and practical Christian theologian. Unknowing but not unwilling, I was finding myself on this journey of awakening to a way of the heart, a path of devotion in conscious love by means of companionship across irreconcilable difference. Step by step, I knew I was going where it felt lively to go. In very real ways, the betrayal that I sense so deeply is completely impersonal. I can offer what I have learned because of the family, ecclesial, and academic life I know, have worked hard for, have been given. Yet we have also been betrayed by ages of refusal and fear, when we persist in not seeing our interconnection and the overwhelming violence against women and children. Our world is groaning under it.

Fruit of many years, then, *A Companionable Way* invites each of us into this way of the heart toward an expressive delight able to companion the suffering of self and others, a way that invites deepening of the journey in which you have been steeped, or been scarred, probably both. I've now unpacked a lot of boxes. Some I knew I was unpacking. Others fell off the truck and spilled open as I stayed at it. I have made a preliminary order of most of the pieces, picking up what has been fruitful and relinquishing that which seems too heavy to carry or impractical for the journey. I will show you what I am taking with me in my knapsack, and you are welcome to any of it that you desire.

Introduction

A Bit on Terms: "Deep Feeling" and "Container"

A couple of observations about some words in the pages to come. *Deep feeling* as I use it here is a primarily relational, embodied, and intuitive force within each of us, including inarticulate and articulate awareness of emotions, sensations, intuitions, hunches and more. It is not solely or even necessarily a conscious force, though it can become so. This force labors—or we labor with it—in resistance and neglect, at the bounds of consciousness. It has great potential for self- and other-transfiguration for the common good. I awakened to it at about age six or seven in an embodied but necessarily hidden way, in my body-dissociated Pennsylvania Deutsch family. It was an awakening to the overwhelming sensation the human body is capable of, interconnected with the mind but also beyond it. The manner in which this occurred, and the isolation in which it occurred, insured that this holy capacity within me would remain in the dark, entangled in shame for decades. Maturing into an adult with it, within a Protestant religiosity that disdains the body—all bodies, especially women's bodies—made it a burden for a long time. It's been this journey—repression, maturation, regression, then regeneration in spirit[5]—that has returned me to *deep feeling* as gift, not burden; invitation, not danger.

The force of deep feeling, finally birthed into my conscious awareness and shared for nearly a decade now with spirit-friends, has been complicated and complicating, of course. By definition, it is exquisitely *intimate* in a world forgetting the nature of authentic intimacy rooted in shared vulnerability. It is excruciatingly *personal*, rooted in the mundane and concrete details of any one and all of our lives—the extraordinary within the cover of the ordinary. This also means it is unavoidably *embodied*, which is befuddling for increasingly disembodied, technological, consumer-driven human beings today, disconnected from the land, geography, earth. Even naming the body means we think it's about sex, when it is not.

To make matters worse for receptivity in this world, coming into deep feeling that is intimate, contextual, and embodied requires a coming to consciousness of an unspoken, perhaps even unspeakable *woundedness* within each of us. Many traditions of religious hue jump on this reality as *sin*, *sinfulness*, even *depravity* deep within us as human beings. On the one hand, it's hard to dispute the evidence—watch the evening news, or witness the vitriol overflowing in the blogosphere. Yet those words do not

---

5. Washburn, *Embodied Spirituality*, 28–31.

describe the woundedness I mean. Honoring its wordless character, I will not presume to name it. I *can* say this *woundedness* began at birth for each of us. Out of our sustained refusal or chosen unconsciousness of it, we use the evidence of the wound to deepen it more, to pretend and defend against it, its cleansing, its healing. No one wants to see, let alone know and feel deeply, this woundedness within. Without redress, we continue to cloak conceptual and physical violence with paternalistic, shaming, systemic attempts of avoidance, neglect. Sustaining ourselves this way while exploiting the world in avoidant fashion, we continue to hold onto impossible certainties and an elitist expertise for the few.

What is ultimately invited in a return to and healthy stewardship of *deep feeling* is an energy, form, and direction able to balance, hold, and nourish. When we are willing to return, to steward, to trust, we receive all the world pours into us in a way more and more necessary for any new life in community to root and blossom today. Stronger, grounded, and circle-way communities are the only containers I know able to hold the deep feeling of each of us in the co-created presence of the greater whole.

Container is another word used in a potentially unfamiliar way in these pages, though more and more folks I encounter are using it in the fashion I intend. Here, it describes the way we structure our communities, our shared time, even our words and our habits of mind, which are the "conceptual containers" in which we understand our world. Our public and private institutions today demonstrate a fairly common shape and energy, at least on the surface. Walk into most civic settings or churches or synagogues today, particularly traditional or (Christian) megachurches, and you'll experience a container with a clear front, perhaps a stage, a body, and a back. It could be represented by a square, a rectangle, or even a lopsided pentagram, but there is a clear hierarchy or point of focus within such a container. Leadership speaks from up front, whether one or a few, and the rest of the gathered listen and act as they are led within social and liturgical customs (now breaking down). The leader can see the most faces, and those gathered can see just a few, unless they twist and turn to look. The cornered-container holds the words and visions of the few, within the silences of the many, at least until one of the larger community pays the cost to become set apart to lead within aging structures that *can* disempower the many.

On the other hand, smaller communities within or outside of these institutions often gather in a differently styled container, best represented

Introduction

by a circle. Emergent communities within religious traditions, for one. Or grass-roots communities in politics. *This* container brings a different archetypal, social energy to the fore when human beings gather together. Requiring smaller numbers, by virtue of its shape, the circle places those gathered such that each person can see the faces of all the others. There is a center in which no one stands, with which everyone can make a direct connection. There *is* no top or bottom, so equity arises more easily. Not assuredly, of course, as it takes intention and practice. There *is* a circle-holder/decision-maker, but the energy of the container is one of co-creation, transparency, accountability, responsibility for self and other. More than just an arrangement of chairs in a room, the circle is an ancient-new *container* inviting a new way—to us today, at least—to be with one another in a collective form, energy, purpose. Mary Pierce Brosmer, founder of Women Writing for (a) Change, defines "container" as the "organizational universe, encompassing all aspects of how a group lives: time, physical space, money, relational agreements, food, and ritual. . . . Anything that maintains the delicate balance between open spaces and boundaries and allows life to emerge." She offers analogues too: "eco-system, home, womb."[6] She gives the story and practices undergirding this circle-way community, a community intent upon conscious care of its container—its light, its shadow, its integrity and rootedness in the world.

In sum, a school could be considered a container, as could a congregation. Most often, however, these are organizational universes unto themselves, unconscious of the smaller "containers" within them or the feared "containers" outside them that require skills, practices, and deep listening to truly hold the words, energies, and deep feeling of their participants. We are largely conditioned in cornered containers to look to the leader(s), to those outside ourselves who we think are responsible for the community life, who are paid or trained to offer us what we need. In these pages, I use the word *container* to refer to the co-created shapes and energies in which people gather to be in community, consciously practicing and deepening the skills and listening necessary to be healthy, more whole, more and more conscious, regardless of their received notions of leadership. An aim of this entire project is for more of us to become more conscious and intentional in the containers to which we accord authority, in which we participate, which hold what is most sacred to us. We need to ask: are these "containers" serving us, *each and all* of us, well?

---

6. Brosmer, *Women Writing for (a) Change*, 182.

A COMPANIONABLE WAY

CONCLUSION

Part memoir, part toolbox, *A Companionable Way* charts one woman's journey of awakening to the deep feeling of devotion in conscious love, possible only with an integrative journey of both light and dark, healed and held by companions from all walks of life, sharing their own charisms as I offered my own. Here you receive stories of my running sacred and scared, of the 18-wheeler of higher-ed expertise I have been trained to drive in the consciousness with which I was shaped. Here you see traditional theological education "stall" in the driveway of a colonial estate, unable to move forward or backward. I am still the Chalcedonian-Christian practical theology professor and Presbyterian "teaching elder" I was. But now, I am also a woman of sacred flesh healed in the gaze of devotion, held in circle-way communities of practice strong enough to hold both light and dark, silence and word, joy and outrage. I am a deeply traditioned woman who was given herSelf—or found herself reborn—only when I was grounded in exile, a befriended outsider, a theist at home in non- or no-theisms, a woman reborn in a circle of wilding women. My "community of faith" lives and breathes outside of, underneath, and within the reigning habits of mind in the institutions I continue to serve. My deepest yearnings to be truly seen, heard, and received just as I am *and* as I continue to grow are met regularly with a love that liberates.

The genre of this kind of life requires your own willingness and intuition, your soul's tenacity to hold onto yourself, allowing your world to unravel a little so it may be reknit, stronger than it ever was. Each "section" of the book offers a story of encounter with challenge to my own yearnings and habits of mind to hold them. A refrain invites you to pause, to ask yourself how the story landed in your body, what (if any) feeling arose in encounter with your own yearnings, habits of mind, received interpretations. Each section then concludes with a more interpretive chapter, offering the sense-making I have crafted for my own balance in this journey of devotion in conscious love.

In the end, you yourself will decide how you awaken to your own deep feeling (or not), how you see the containers in your life that hold you, and what sense you will make of your own yearnings and habits of mind. To return to the original image: a companionable way of being in the world takes jumping down from the truck and sustaining a bit of jarring awareness. All you need is a box-cutter, a knapsack, curiosity, and a willingness to enter into a journey where you take responsibility for your choiceless choices,

INTRODUCTION

you bring only what both nourishes and challenges you, with neither sacrificed for the other. You will find what your heart desires most deeply. You can learn to companion suffering within an abundance that cannot be shaken. No one need carry everything for themselves when a circle community holds a wholeness greater than its parts. Select and carry what you need. Be willing to share what you have in abundance. Your companions will find you.

Grounding in Exile

A companionable way of being was seeded in my life when I, a theological professor and preacher's wife, was manhandled at an after-church coffee hour. I marvel at this today, how significantly this brief, painful event instigated so much that I now cherish in my life. I have made a lot of lemonade with this lemon. Propelled away from the pain, I landed in a nonlinear, spiral path of awakening, self-discovery, and forgiveness. I came to know the gifts that find you in exile, if you learn how to look for them. Even when the pain of departure overwhelms everything you thought you knew, wondrous light, love, and levity can await you too.

The story can be told in a sentence and a poem. A longtime class clown and devout elder of my husband's church, "Jim," ass-slapped me twice at coffee hour.

> "We have pound-cake to tempt you,"
> he said to her in the Ann Taylor suit.
> "Vanilla for this side," slapping her ass.
> "Chocolate for that one." Ass-slapped again.
>
> He looked around the church for others
> to join the fun. Only a young girl across
> the table stared back at him. She vanished
> in place, there but not there. A hole where
>
> a heart had been. The other shell of a woman?
> She walked out alone. Her husband, the pastor,
> was everywhere, so nowhere. Wounded too,
> though absent. Pain for the journey had come.

These lines—three stanzas about two jarring slaps—arose years ago as poetic truth-telling for me, struggling to know how to respond gracefully, strategically, and faithfully to an embarrassing violation of my own bodyspace in the environment of my husband's job, part of our economic livelihood and perceived sacred calling. For years, we kept quiet about any of it, amidst the familiar setting of a traditional church coffee hour where good-hearted people gather with one another each week to listen to one another's lives. The images could bring a whiff of the Three Stooges or a bit of slapstick Charlie Chaplin, if the intersection of a woman's body and old-boy religion weren't still so tender. For five years, the places of home, church, and work could not hold this splinter of the flesh, this all too familiar story of a woman handled, humiliated, and silenced. It still reigns in me to downplay its significance, say it didn't matter, *when it does, it did*. Within two years, I rarely visited my husband's congregation, finding sanctuary and deepening faith practice with a local Tibetan Buddhist sangha closer to our home.

I'm not the first woman nor the last who has such a story of body handling and dissociation, holding it quiet for years. No spaces or shapes of community life had been available to me to become conscious that such an event mattered enough to merit anger aloud. I hear worse stories every time deeply reflective women gather together, conscious about their own well-being in the world. These stories need telling, for however long women and men need to awaken to the fact that they matter. But for five years, my husband and I, my immediate family, my church community absented ourselves from the knowledge that I and my experience as a woman could matter more than keeping the peace with a pound-cake perpetrator of old-boy civic religion.

Two marriages received scars here while home stretched painfully across church and work. For mine, my husband was secretly outraged, holding the toxicity deep within himself without my knowledge for nearly four years. As pastors, we both felt he was disempowered to respond without destabilizing his new role in ministry, which neither of us desired. We therefore *both* abandoned our experiences. While my Buddhist practice deepened and I served various congregations in adult education and pulpit supply, "church" became an empty space of formality and civic rite for me, weighted to irrelevance in its need for palatable public truth. Simultaneously, a spiritual friendship began in my life, moving my life into congregational exile, with salve beyond ecclesial norms. Companionships outside the structures of church began to hold the healing in a way the ecclesial structures were unable. Strangely liberated, then, I *did* become free to move outward—even as far as the Tibetan center—to find new sacred relationships outside of all my own traditioned shapes of community.

After those five years, as I found my way into circle-way communities of practice, as I was held by spiritual friends deeply rooted in their own wisdom traditions, way did open to tell gently the truth of my experience. The Wednesday of Holy Week, my husband-the-pastor and I visited "Jim" and his wife, in their living room. I brought a box of poundcake with the request that he receive it from me, that they listen while I told the story that had instigated a painful but now beautiful exile from congregational settings. I think each of us in the room, except Jim perhaps, finally saw the collision of small-town culture, urban professionalism in a woman, and unfortunate happenstance. He denied it. His wife cried. The pastor prayed for healing afterwards, and Easter Sunday beckoned to us all. As was my habit on those "nonnegotiable Sundays" I had to be there, I arrived late. This time, I noticed an open seat right next to Jim and his wife. I smiled, feeling tender but also open. I sat down next to them, and when it was time for communion, we walked up to the sacrament together, the frail and reconciled human beings that we were. Jim and his wife then became two of my favorite people in the church, as the theological reality about which I teach and in which I serve had been lived and shared by the four of us.

So, far from just the familiar story of a woman wounded by an unthinking man in a religious tradition, this event became seed of my own exile, an awakening to an undesired but unavoidable invitation outward into other communities, other practices. I found myself on a deepening path of darkness and light within which the Sacred could arise anew between those willing to journey together beyond familiar shapes of home, work, and church/tradition. New friends pushed me into a holy meander . . . into Tibetan Buddhist practices, Jewish hospitality and observance, Muslim *salat*, coffee cups with atheists, practices with earth-centered and woman-centric communities. We journey-folks are many now, immersed in companionable practices and circle learnings, finding one another along the way, learning together how to hold the "too muchness" of injuries of tribalism with compassion, integrity, and humility. This splinter of the flesh, goading me outward, slowly became a story of commitment to the way and shape that *can* hold dark and light long enough for a journey of healing, abundance, and reconciliation to be borne: a *circle*.

Pain hurts, but it need not become (or remain) suffering. Salve comes when you seek it, whether you're aware of seeking or not. Rooted within my own tradition, I'd even say *salvation* comes as suffering softens the heart, opens it for healing, and, when way opens, wholeness is found. There is no excuse for the behavior named in this church coffee hour, man to woman, but there is (now) seasoned empathy and self-compassion, which extends then to compassion for Jim too. We are sparks of the divine *and* shells of fearful division. Separate from one another, we injure one another, sometimes with intention, often without. Opened to wisdom, stumbling toward interdependence, we glimpse a better way. The pain of this event pushed me into exile. Deep inner work and gracious companionship from *outside* allowed me freedom to see, to be seen, to tell the truth, and to forgive. Grounding in exile.

A Companionable Way

How might your life have been different . . .
    if your place in the world felt safe, regardless of who you are,
        you knew you belonged, assured, just as you are . . .

    if public and private truths stood next to one another,
        honoring the gifts of each?

    if injury did not hide in shame but was offered
        for the purification and transfiguration of each,
            if and when the injured were willing?

    if the sacred did not shield us from the fears of men
       nor hide the dignity and wisdom of women,
            hidden deeply within the unconscious, unwelcome and denied
                until safe space is held to bring this wordlessness to voice?

            How might your life have been different?
            How might our world be different?

Desire

"We're never going to use this," responded a student to the end-of-semester discussion in my interreligious-intercultural methods class, a master's course crafted to shape peaceable and impassioned faith encounters in the ministries of fledgling religious leaders. "We don't even have a Catholic church in town, let alone a synagogue, mosque, or temple. We're never going to use this." I was stunned, and not a little stung. How could that possibly be true? How could he not see the value in *learning how to learn about one another across difference*, learning to actively love one another across culture and tradition? Does he not live in the same world that the rest of us do? Does he not encounter political refugees and immigrants around every grocery store aisle?

Blunt honesty stings, which is why so few of us offer it to one another. When received with curiosity and an ability to hold negative energies, his words eventually showed me what I had refused to see. Because he was absolutely right. He and his words reminded me of a portion of the American population increasingly misunderstood or misperceived within discourse and media attentive to other concerns. He spoke as a leader in a community disenchanted with industrial agriculture, technological overwhelm, and globalization. He spoke as one whose lived reality is one of more oral communication than literate—which is not to say an illiterate community, just one less inclined to receive information or news from print media. He spoke of a large population often defensive against or "unplugged" from what appears to some of us as an unavoidable global village. Just because religious pluralism and cultural diversity are touted both directly and indirectly from ivory tower and multimedia outlets does not mean that this diversity informs everyone's daily lives. One (or many) *can* choose to craft a reality that diminishes pluralisms, avoids diversity, regulates the most important fundamentals. Diversity's prevalence does *not* mean that all of us *have* to confront it regularly. Yet.

MOVING THE DISCOURSE INWARD

As with many hot-button issues in our day, there seem to be those who find diversity an unadulterated good, evidence of the mystery of infinite creativity. "We" are the ones who urge progressive reform of political and religious institutions, who attempt to open doors that slam in the faces of those who do not look like us or believe as we do. We think everyone should learn skills of peace-filled community building across diversity lines. Then there are those who find this diversity to be an unadulterated bad, a threat to the unity of community, belief, practice or tradition—with its complex interrelations of all those things. "We" are the ones who rightly see the diminishment of life we hold sacred, the relativism of what's most important toward the flatness of what is most common. Instead, we see our lives as ones of integrity, commitment in the face of opposition, truth in the face of the common denominator attempting to make us all the same—those attempting to say these sacred things don't matter, are not sacred.

Of course, these "those" are caricatures of various polarized adjectives—liberal/conservative, progressive/traditional, etc.—purported to be addressed and redressed with scholarship on religious pluralism, interfaith and/or interreligious concerns. Most everyone willing to talk about these things knows that diversity is neither an unadulterated good nor an unadulterated bad. It is complicated. Even so, all this brought a new question into my awareness, a question of *willingness* and *desire*. I began to see a need to awaken to "ourselves" anew in an increasingly fearful world of "other." We need to relearn something so basic as how to see more of what is, to perceive without evaluation or judgment, instead of seeing as we have been shaped by those closest to us.

The literatures on religious pluralism, interreligious dialogue, interfaith service, and more develop exponentially by the year, if not by the month. The able work of Diana Eck and the Pluralism Project[1] ought not to be underestimated for its contributions, nor should any other seriously critical engagement with today's complexities: academic disciplines like theologies of religious pluralism, comparative theology, and scriptural reasoning. The inquiry broadens, as it does, and the disciplines specialize,

---

1. Eck, *A New Religious America*. See also www.pluralism.org.

as they do. Other figures drawn into cross-pollinating work—Joan Chittister, for example—offer expansive texts rooted more in story and wisdom distilled in their travels: *The Tent of Abraham: Stories of Hope and Peace for Jews, Christians, and Muslims* (written in collaboration with Murshid Saadi Shakur Chishti and Rabbi Arthur Waskow) or *Welcome to the Wisdom of the World and Its Meaning for You*, for example. Everyone who writes in this field, as I have engaged it, is so far into the work that the actual motivations and the desire to engage can often be presumed. Willingness and desire must both be functioning in order to come to fruition in a book or extended writings.

One of the most recent resources illustrating this conundrum comes through Kristin Johnston Largen, in collaboration with Mary E. Hess and Christy Lohr Sapp. She begins with the question, "How interreligious is your life?"[2] and then argues for how implicitly interreligious our world is, whether we are aware of it or not. She examines and wrestles with four practical situations worth your pursuit, if interested: the practice of yoga, the media stunt of Qur'an burning, Buddhist meditation, and the growing trend of "Christian" Seders. She offers an excellent Christian rationale for engagement with interreligious learning, with careful attention to "praxis points" and practical reflection questions. She seems to feel the same urgency I do about a more expansive sense of *community* and the role of the body in finding a more companionable way to be with those outside our traditions' identities. But who will pick up a book on "encountering otherness," on interreligious learning, except those already so inclined? While I am interested in the arena of interreligious and intercultural encounters, I'm actually *more* interested in something deeply rooted in each of us, no matter our tradition (or none).

DESIRE FOR AWAKENING TO THE UNEXPECTED IN A VIOLENT, FEARFUL WORLD

My beloved student's bald statement—"We're never going to use this"—brought me up short with a much more elemental question I now need to ask: How *do* we awaken desire for deepening in a world so captivated by fear and violence, particularly as the deepening may be not what we desire or expect? *How do we awaken desire for unexpected and uncontrolled encounters with any and all those in our "global village" whose lives are hidden*

---

2. Largen, Hess, and Sapp, *Interreligious Learning and Teaching*, 1.

from each other, from us, whether by hardened intention or unintentional circumstance?

I suppose you could also ask it this way: if you are a seeker, how do you see those who are not seeking (as you are) with compassion? How do you hold your own fear and frustration that "they" do not find your seeking faithful or they refuse to venture outside their own safety zones? How do you awaken desire to see this "other" anew, again and again, even when s/he angers, frustrates, even enrages you? Or perhaps you are one of those who feel this deep certainty, even absolute assurance, in your beliefs. What gifts are seekers bringing for you? What does their spirit have to teach you? How do *we* awaken desire to see anew in a world of fear and violence?

These questions are much more ubiquitous, and much more urgent, than I first supposed. My first associations as I listened to these voices were those of an analytical academic greatly surprised at rurally shaped human worldviews, habits of mind. I admit the words "ignorant" and "sheltered" came to mind. "Out of touch" and "lack of civic responsibility" weren't far behind. How could it not be obvious that the world needs to learn peaceful behaviors of coexistence across cultural and religious diversities . . . and that means us, you, me? Of course, these things tell you more about *me* than anything about them. I have a decade-long growth spurt unfolding in me in my journey from establishment academic at a prestigious institution of higher learning on the East Coast to a small, struggling institution of higher education in the Midwest. It's been a rough road to see as children of God all those whose politics and felt-rigid religion make my blood boil. I dare anyone in a progressive-liberal urban enclave to come and live in these shoes for a couple of years.

Simultaneously, I'm inexpressibly grateful for this "rough" road, this path that has opened doors more intellectually stimulating and ripe with contribution than those of golden-handcuffed provision and Christian-privileged, largely white guilt. Perhaps *rough* is not the right word for the road. Adventurous, exotic, stimulating, enraging, instructive, humbling . . . *awakening* myself. You see, if one listens with attention to hearing and seeing God's voice through *every* person, what Christians call "the Christ within," one can begin to hear without judgment the necessary information for better teaching, broader contribution, and new directions of inquiry. As I relinquished my academic disbelief at the student's words, I began to see a sad truism for many more communities of faith than just those my students serve. "We're never going to use this" could be stated by just about any mainline congregational community today—Christian, Jewish, Muslim, and more (who are willing to be referenced as a "congregation")—or any community with an identity or resources to protect.

STRUCTURAL OBSTACLES TO AWAKENING

Amidst the overwhelming changes and increased encounter with "otherness" of all kinds, most faith communities gather to reaffirm their own rooted identities in traditions persistently attempting to resist diffusion, relativism, and syncretism. If and when attention is left over for "otherness," then interfaith or interreligious concerns may arise. Or when a civic holiday arrives, like Martin Luther King Jr. Day. Or anniversaries like 9/11. On those two or three days a year, communities divert attention to such interreligious concerns for a moment. Specifically inter*cultural* diversities may arise in the context of mission trips—groups going on a mission to another country—or when welcoming a missionary from another country who is traveling to share teachings and raise funds. Otherwise, and I say this without blame, most faith communities I know—even the most progressive ones—are not hotbeds of interreligious encounter of any overt or concrete kind. They could easily say, "We're never going to use this." The purpose or mission in religiously identified communities is not interreligious or intercultural encounter but proclaiming the gospel, or loving one's neighbor, or serving Christ, or bringing the Dharma to the West (Buddhist), or worshipping the One G-d, or (insert mission statement here). Religious communities are, by traditional definition and practice, predisposed to *under*value interreligious and intercultural exploration in structural, functional ways.

In speech, we want to encounter "others." In communal self-perceptions, we are open-hearted, open-minded. But in structural ways, in daily or weekly practices of concrete action? That's not what church (or synagogue, or mosque, or . . .) is *for*. We want "others" to come to us, to fit within our own comfort zones. "Visitors welcome," we say. Where do you read or hear, "We are willing to encounter you as you are, where you are, receiving you and demanding nothing of you but to listen, to learn, to welcome change"? This second statement is simply too long for a church sign and would be considered unfaithful in any synagogue or mosque newsletter.

A mentor-teacher, Fred Craddock, paints a good picture of what I now see. Ever curious about new approaches to old classics—like rhetoric, preaching, argument—Craddock decided to shadow a renowned college

English teacher at the local university for a day, to see what he might learn about teaching. The last class of the day was a senior seminar, twelve or so students gathered around John Donne's metaphysical poetry and one student's sustained argument presented as a paper. The professors sat in the middle of the table, watching the conceptual ping-pong matches begin, with volleys and lobs thrown in nearly every direction. When one seemed to lose its momentum, the professor would lend a new one to the discourse and the play would begin again.

The first class of the day, however, had been English 101, 8:30 a.m., a large auditorium for a class of 250, mostly freshmen. Bleary-eyed young men shuffled in, some still wearing their pajamas and slippers; a newspaper raised from the penultimate row in the back. Young women and men flocked in, dispersing in almost polar-opposite magnetic fashion, randomly but with expansive space between gathered clusters. The professor began with some informal conversation with students in the front row. Chatty pre-class things, seemingly without intention. Someone told a joke and the professor laughed, parrying with another. The students in the first several rows began to get involved. Class began seamlessly, with American literature finding its way in historical perspective, gaining momentum in energy until the newspapers came down in the back. "What's he saying?" one asked. Class had finally, completely begun.

Craddock reflected with his professorial colleague on the pedagogies involved in these vastly different teaching-learning environments. The professor noted it in terms of desire. The senior seminar *assumes* the desire, builds upon it, moves it deeper and broader with collaborative engagement of texts. The introductory class, however, cannot assume such desire. It must be built up in each class, created anew in each session, often using new and different techniques each time.

Our institutional containers and the discourses they harbor are not designed to foster or sustain desire for peaceable encounters across difference, with deep feelings arising in a world increasingly fearful and violent. Most discourse in this area of inquiry essentially assumes outer need and inner desire for interreligious or intercultural encounter are the same thing, or interchangeable. The rationale comes almost as trope by now: Diversity is undeniable. We see war and violence every day, much of it in religious dress (or drag). Therefore, interreligious and intercultural learning is warranted, necessary, an obligation or duty. Desire to be engaged must arise from this portrait of the world.

Except willingness and desire don't operate like that, especially when fear and violence are prevalent and deep feeling is largely unaddressed. Most folks I encounter express little or no desire for finding an "other" outside their current worldviews or expectations. We see through the lenses we're given, barely awake to the reality that we *have* lenses, and often averse to the notion of taking the lenses off or putting on new ones. Many of us have been taught that cultivating such desire or willingness to seek, to find, is a faithless endeavor—it suggests lack of belief, integrity, commitment to one's heritage, tradition, God, and more. So we return to our question, intended for many more of us than "those people": *How do we awaken desire for encounter across difference with those in our "global village" whose lives are hidden from each other, whether by hardened intention or unintentional circumstance?*

This question also honors the hardened intentions, which are probably there for good reason, if others are willing to listen. Fundamentalists irritate, even enrage, but if you look and listen long enough, the need for such structure, such so-called rigidities, may eventually make some sense. Yes, fundamentalists can be dangerous, and responses we have are violence to violence. But even asking the question accords value and honoring of the intentional and unintentional circumstances folks find themselves in too. Seeing the circumstances of "others"—whether described in geographical (urban, suburban, exurban, rural), economic (1 percent, 99 percent; rich, middle class, working poor, poor), ethnic, cultural, racial, gender, sexual orientation, or other terms—may help more of us hold strong enough spaces for such pain and outrage. It's hard to hate a person whose story you know.

Desire is also a term rife with misunderstanding, fear, and violence. What does healthy desire look like in a culture obsessed with sexual desire alone? What about passion to create, to heal, to hold broader community than one's own in mysteries unfathomed by you before? Do many of us actually want to awaken to the kind of desire that makes us vulnerable, shows our own limitations, opens us to what we cannot name? Psychological forces defend persons' views and minds for good reason, most especially those unready to be vulnerable in ways others may want them to be. Busting through psychological defenses is still violent, if in a different way than bulldozing the walls of someone's house.

"We are never going to use this." Perhaps. Willingness and desire are delicate matters of chosen vulnerability, readiness, and inner strength to withstand all we cannot control in honesty, integrity, and hope. Finding the pathway to peaceable encounter needs to arise in as much gentle awakening as we can muster, while attuned to the urgency and need in our world for new ways of being human together, with, and for one another. I know few disciplinary rationales that will open hearts like that, nor are the containers in our religious communities, schools, or government well suited to deep feeling work. Stories in invitational prose may be our best opportunity to awaken desire—indirectly, without agenda, open to encounter just as we are. A companionable way of being in the world begins with stories that invite deepening inner work in us all.

Deep Roots in Difference

He filled the cup to overflowing, right there at the dinner table. The red wine held itself at the lip of the cup for as long as it could, then overflowed onto the plate below, as it did every Friday night in this home. I felt tears of recognition and wonder begin to bubble up within me. A psalm rose loud and strong in my awareness—the Twenty-Third Psalm, in the King James poetry I memorized when I was young: "You set a table before me . . . you anointest my head with oil; my cup runneth over. Surely goodness and mercy shall follow me all the days of my life: and I will dwell in the house of the LORD forever." Embarrassed at such emotional display that night, I tried covertly to wipe the tears from my eyes. I had just met this rabbi and his wife fifteen minutes before, yet they had welcomed me into their home for Shabbat. I felt foolish, but I also sensed a fierce Presence among us. Shmuel was singing the blessing over the cup, the kiddush, and the challot (two loaves), prepared especially for this day, were waiting. The Sabbath Queen had arrived and we were all within her cloak of celebration.

The road traveled to this moment had been bumpy, to say the least. I had received a mean-spirited e-mail from a professional Jewish acquaintance who had felt slighted. The internal community work of new curriculum development had completely overwhelmed me, requiring all my focus. Interfaith work external to my seminary teaching had taken a lower priority, resulting in a perceived slight and disrespect. The nonviolent communication work of Marshall Rosenberg saved the day, which led to three e-mails to Jewish and Muslim practitioners involved in the local trialogue community. Though on the cusp of the Jewish holidays, I wrote a newsy, rather impish self-introduction and invitation to tea to each of them. Rabbi Shmuel, now a dear friend, wrote back almost immediately. "I would be delighted. After the holidays, please come to my home to celebrate Shabbat with my wife and me. Shall we set the date?" I was stunned, and not a little scared. We Presbyterians start slow, work up speed and intimacy if and when "it goes well," whatever that might mean. I have several close friends within my own faith tradition who have never been to my home, for instance. Shmuel and Naomi went straight for the highest point of hospitality in my world: visiting in the home of a stranger. I was excited and terrified.

The day of the Shabbat dinner arrived. My husband and I combed Internet sources to find out whether it was "kosher" to bring a host gift, and if so, *what?* Was it work on the Sabbath to cut stems of fresh flowers? Would we be able to bring something edible for a Chabad couple of ultra-Orthodox observance? We elected to bring flowers, hoping for the best. As I knocked on the door, I remembered: Hasidic rabbis (rebbes) do not shake hands with women. "Don't put your hand out to shake his hand," I reminded myself. Shmuel met us at the door with a huge grin. "Welcome!" he said, bringing his right hand up to his forehead in a playful salute. "We call this the 'rabbi salute.' I am so glad you are here." I eased instantly, and something deep within me opened. *He's done this so many times. I feel like I know him already.* I laughed at the rabbi salute and said how tickled we were to be welcomed into his home. "Shall we move to the table?" he asked, gesturing to the dining room where the best china and silverware were laid out on placemats. Two loaves of challah peeked out from under a brocade cover or cloth, and the red wine bottle rested next to his plate. A small silver cup rested on a small plate, next to the wine. As this new, felt-friend began to sing the blessing over the cup, my own tears began to bubble up.

This evening also planted a seed that was to sprout two weeks later, as a new friend, Brad Hirschfield, a Modern Orthodox rabbi, would be leading a largely Methodist Christian community in a theology course and then worship service, followed by a common meal. When the Christian liturgy concluded, Brad stood at a small table alongside me. He wanted to model the Shabbat table practices of his own community. While he sang the blessing over the cup, both he and I filled two separate chalices to overflowing, just as Shmuel had—but this time, one with kosher wine, the other with grape juice. Together, but also separate; connected, yet also different. A loaf of bread was distributed to those gathered amidst a wordless Hebrew tune, and then our whole community's common meal began. We shared in table fellowship, Brad with his own kosher-prepared meal.

With great care to our respective traditions—what we could do with authority and what needed to be resisted for sake of integrity—this event of "liturgical hospitality" was the most eucharistic event of my entire ministry life. Neither Shabbat nor Eucharist, neither separatist Christian nor defensive Jewish, some pattern of the Holy found its way into a ritual gathering and time of informal table fellowship. A poem arrived later, while sitting back in the Marianist grotto that afternoon:

> Two cups filled to overflowing.
> Roshi observes that fullness obstructs.
> Rebbe shows a fullness that welcomes.
> Roshi pours hot water from teacup to table.
> The student awakens, disturbed to learn emptiness.
> Rebbe pours a care-full wine, just as the psalmist says.
> The student awakens, startled with Life set apart.
> Such liturgical hospitality disturbs and disrupts
> What we cannot abandon or alter,
> Healing through yearnings well met,
> Blessing the unbidden tears.
> A pastor and rabbi attended a table,
> Two cups filled to overflowing.

This stream of events opened my mind and heart to the mystery of spiritual maturity and the risks of faith in liturgical innovation required to hold and be held within spiritual friendships amidst historic wisdom traditions. Both Brad and I bow to the woundedness that so often overwhelms intertraditional discourse *and* we are entrusted with leadership in our respective sacred traditions. The events were not intentional, nor are they prescriptive. Neither he nor I know traditional language to use for it but that which we have, halakah and Presbyterian polity that governed our actions. We are intimately aware of the sustained paradoxes amidst irreconcilable difference.

Yet we, and those who participated that day, were willing to live in the tension of this sustained paradox, in engagement, long-term aspiration, and even a willingness to suffer for God's life to grow more fully in each and all of us. We were drawn to the possibility that an original *covenant of beholding*[1]—holding and being held in scriptural, deeply sacred but unexpected ways—could create spacious ways for us to rest firm within our traditionally defined senses of covenant, however singular, however multiple, while belonging deeply to one another across traditionally defined categories of any tradition.

---

1. Ross, *Writing the Icon*, xviii.

With all of my intertraditional collaborations across various traditions and non-traditions (Tibetan Buddhism, various streams of Judaism, Divine Feminine, pagan, atheist, Muslim, and more), I have rarely been companioned myself, at the center of my tradition, at *Eucharist*. There are all kinds of reasons I sense for this, not least of which is a cultural-Christian colonialism-imperialism that needs rebalancing. One Wednesday morning, after Brad and I had sat on a panel discussing relationship across theological difference, we sat in my office as communal worship began. He inquired whether we ought to be present *there*, and I relented, uneasy with the liturgical focus of the day—evangelism and "Offer Them Christ." We had laughed about it together, but I was deeply uneasy as a Christian welcoming a Jew into such a setting. As the liturgy moved into the sacramental celebration at table, I mourned that he would never be with me at the center of *my* tradition. Deeply grieving, I approached the table to receive, still to give thanks to God for such abundance that was and is mine, and yes, to bring my sadness to this center of my own tradition. As I turned to walk back to my seat, my eyes landed on him, sitting in a posture of devotion and prayer, deeply present with me, *beholding*. Beholding me, beholding the entire room as we were receiving our sustenance at the heart of Christian practice. He was so clearly present with me, with us, though he did not partake of the sacramental feast prepared. We were both deeply rooted, *and* in our difference.

Deep Roots in Difference

How might your life have been different if, deep within,
    you carried an image of Love that overflowed,
        a feeling of God beyond bounds,
            an offering of Love poured out just for you, for all those wounded?

And when things seemed hopelessly separate and hostile,
    wounded and impossible,
        the gatekeepers of this Love breathed deeply into possibility,
            willing to sustain the ire of "their own" in order to love *you*,
                to behold you, to cherish you, embraced at last?

And that you could hear a Voice saying to you
    I love you . . . and you and you and you . . .
        I love each of you and I *need* you to bring forth my Life.
        Do not fear: I am sending you just who you will need . . .

            How might your life be different?
            How might our world be different?

Liturgical Hospitality

Historic traditions within communities of practice today center most often in the liturgical life shared weekly on Sunday mornings, Saturday mornings, Friday afternoons, or other times, depending upon tradition. *A Companionable Way* found one of its seeds in a specifically liturgical event, though the pathway to understanding required a bit of cross-traditional expertise and collaborative listening. What follows here is the "comparative theology" sense-making required for deep roots in difference. There is a stronger attention to texts and to discourse, given the sensitivity of the subject. But the irrevocable force of Love and Life cannot be ignored or dissuaded from disrupting any/all attempts to imprison it—including precious, holy sacraments.

Ordinary life can be the most extraordinary, as any contemplative will tell you. It speaks a liminal logic, if you know how to see, to look for it. I find this to be much like the hidden patterning of time and action at the heart of an unprogrammed Quaker meeting, which does have an implicit rhythm and order to it each time. I'm most familiar with the overt "order of worship" in mainline Protestant settings, of course. Such are the shapes of my traditioned experiences well into adulthood, sculpting my expectation and experience of the Holy. Led and accompanied by willing interfaith companions, I eventually found this liminal logic in my rabbi friends' teaching acts of sanctification, in our shared acts of remembrance and observation, even in Christian sacramental beholding, if not participation. All of this has led to a rooted and holy devotion, a hasidism or piety overflowing into thanksgiving and joy among spirit-friends across irreconcilable traditions.

Sensitive to the potential for real pain, this chapter explores a "pattern of the holy" as recognized, unexpectedly, within two distinctly established liturgical practices involving a cup filled with the fruit of the vine, shared in a space made sacred before a common meal of table fellowship in a multipurpose space at a Protestant seminary in the Midwest. The intention is to reflect critically upon an intensely felt, potentially significant liturgical "event," which was intentional and unplanned, deeply traditional and unintentionally innovative. What I now understand to have happened here, which I do not recommend now as anything other than the one event it was: a Jewish logic of sanctification, offered in a modeled teaching of the Shabbat eve kiddush, coincided and was interwoven with a Christian sacramental logic upon the conclusion of a formal, Christian "order of worship." A liminal liturgical space (or event of "liturgical reasoning") was therefore created in which neither "rooted practitioner" in leadership relinquished his or her own theological particularity. Both manifested, publicly, a tenacious commitment to lived interdependence in difference.

The comparative work here—brief and incomplete—will begin with examination of the Shabbat eve kiddush in halakic overview, as the originating event was an Orthodox Shabbat eve kiddush. What emerges is what I call a *logic of sanctification*, which overflowed into Christian liturgical practice, thereby enlivening new awareness of an old symbolism within *that* theological tradition. The kiddush cup—with its significations in testimony, sanctification, remembrance, and observance—invites encounter and contrast with the communion chalice of Christian eucharistic practice, rooted in its own *sacramental logic* of creation, incarnation, death, and resurrection life.

The sense of *liturgy* intended for this purpose arises from a conviction grown in these events, then confirmed within recent literature, specifically *Liturgical Reasoning*, by Steven Kepnes. Life-giving, comparative theological work begins with liturgy, not theology or any precise textual study, however important that may become. Teaching religiously homogenous or "superficially traditional," even unconsciously anti-Semitic, students in a Midwestern theological seminary, created the felt-urgency and the context for this conviction. A recent work of Jewish liturgical reasoning has confirmed its viability. Relying upon his work, I will describe liturgy as "a collective activity ... of the present moment that was nevertheless performed in the past." It is "a communal performance of word, text, and song, in a space set apart," in which "the communal body" of practice "becomes the organ of the reasoning" of its theological tradition. It enacts "a sphere in which thinking about primary existential, metaphysical, and theological issues occurs." All of these words have been his, but let us listen to a marvelous image from Steven Kepnes here, cited with some enforced brevity:

> Liturgy is not a passive recipient or mere vessel of reason but ... in liturgy, the ... light of ... reason fans out into a spectrum of colors and hues so that its concepts and ideals are clothed in particular images and displayed in ritual actions.... The clarion call of reason becomes a melody that is varied, repeated, submerged, and revealed anew as in a musical fugue.... [T]he reason of liturgy is temporal and spatial ... it is never the same. Because liturgy is a living performance ..., it always varies from its script. Thus, liturgical reasoning is always new. It is neither preexistent nor static; it is discovered and revealed in every liturgical performance.[1]

Critical distinctions would further refine this inquiry, but for now, suffice to say the event examined here has the hallmarks of "liturgical reasoning"—primarily temporal and spatial, communally enacted. I take responsibility for any imprecision in what is to follow, but I also take courage in Kepnes' approach, as he describes it. "In light of the plethora of dead signs that now litter the sacred spaces of synagogues, liturgical reasoning is an act of breathing new life into old signs. In Jewish liturgical terms, this can be referred to as an act of *Mehiat ha Matim* [sic], reviving the dead."[2] The Christian church is no less littered with "dead signs," and so I pursue this work as a form of "apophatic resurrection life" made available to Protestant (and other interested) Christians within my tradition(s).

A HALAKIC OVERVIEW OF KIDDUSH

We begin with the halakic overview of Shabbat eve kiddush. *Kiddush* describes many things within Orthodox Jewish tradition, but it's probably safe to say it rarely describes what it did that Wednesday morning in a multipurpose space at a Midwestern Protestant seminary. Kiddush (variably pronounced ki-DOOSH or KID-ish) comes from a Hebrew root, *qdsh*, meaning to be made holy, to be set apart, to sanctify/be sanctified. It describes various blessings within Jewish practice, as well as times of table fellowship following Shabbat prayer services. As one wise young woman taught me, "It moves around" in Jewish observance.[3] One could even call it a "coffee hour" within Protestant Christian-speak, but that would be

---

1. Kepnes, *Jewish Liturgical Reasoning*, 3.

2. Ibid., 19. A different rabbinic colleague suggested *Techiyat hameitim* as the correct Hebrew term.

3. Hadassa Hirschfield, conversation, May 23, 2010.

inaccurate, let alone imprecise. In the more precise context of this event and halakic overview, kiddush refers to the opening blessing on Shabbat eve sung over the cup of juice or wine, sometimes over the two challah (or challot), testifying to God as Creator, to God's rest, to the entrance of the Sabbath queen into the lives and homes of the observant. In this kiddush, those gathered before a meal enter into participation in God's rest even as they also fulfill the obligation to "keep the Sabbath," to keep it holy.

Rabbi Adin Steinsaltz describes the setting for this kiddush in popularist terms: "On entering a home on the eve of the Sabbath, one may see how a dwelling is made into a sanctuary. . . . Especially is this true on the Sabbath, when the Sabbath feast takes on the character of a sacramental act, a sort of communion, in the performance of the *mitzvah* of union of the soul, the body, the food, and the essence of holiness."[4] His description relies upon kabbalistic terminology perhaps a little more accessible for a popularist audience. A more rigorous halakic understanding comes through Rabbi Doniel Schreiber of Har Etzion yeshiva, who describes kiddush as the weekly inauguration and sanctification of Shabbat and one of the most festive and celebrated moments in the Jewish family experience.[5] He offers commentary (in translation) upon the Source and Scope of the kiddush, and outlines the procedure from the time for reciting kiddush, through its observant setting and distinguishing elements of practice. In his view, the Shabbat eve kiddush is a testimony to God as Creator whose creation summons in the Sabbath at sundown and whose faithful people sanctify the day in an act of remembrance (*zakhor*) and observance (*shamor*). The central question for halakic discourse in the *mitzvah* of kiddush, according to Rav Yosef Zvi Rimon, is whether "it constitutes a Torah obligation or was instituted later, by Chazal," as a rabbinic institution. Kiddush is therefore a positive obligation fulfilled weekly, whether understood within Torah or rabbinic terms, and is an intimate portion of the (three) meals required/ invited in Jewish observance. My attention remains on the Shabbat eve kiddush, in contrast to "the Great Kiddush" offered on Shabbat day itself. "And God blessed the seventh day, and sanctified it; because in it He rested from all His work that God had created and performed."

Jewish scholars debate whether the saying/singing of kiddush sanctifies the cup, the contents of the cup, the lives of those gathered, or whether it even welcomes the extra souls loaned to the observant for the duration

---

4. Steinsaltz, "Additional Note on the *Kiddush* Ritual," 154.
5. Schreiber, "*Kiddush*: a Halakhic Overview—Part I," 71–84.

of Shabbat. But as the sun sets and brings the Sabbath, it *is* clear to many of the observant that humans have no agency in such sanctification. As a holy act in created time and space, humans simply participate in it in order to observe and remember the Sabbath. Those gathered remember God as Creator who rested. They celebrate creation and enter into God's rest. Perhaps they even see glimpses of the World to Come, and remember who they are as humans, in intimate covenant. The sanctification of the day upon and through the kiddush is an act of the Ancient of Days begun in creation, offered today, providing the essence or taste of the World to Come.

Several distinctions may be useful at this point. In this case, the modeled teaching of a Shabbat table practice on Wednesday morning would not be considered a kiddush within Orthodox Jewish observance. The time was Wednesday noon; the sun was not setting; *ma'ariv* (prayer service) had not been spoken; candles had not been lit; blessings had not been said, nor the woman of the house (or children) blessed. All but one of the participants were not Jewish. A practical theological scholar such as myself would not have had access to even what I have learned so far, except for the technological precision and integrative scholarship of Alei Etzion, an Israeli yeshiva that engages halakah and offers it in translation for broader critical understanding. Any liturgical actions offered on that Wednesday noon, then, are best described as analogically liturgical, not Orthodox observance.

Even so, halakah recognizes that in contrast to the Festivals of Jewish observance, Shabbat has a force apart from human participation and observance.[6] The sanctification of Shabbat fulfilled in the Shabbat eve kiddush is an act of sanctification distinct from any human agency and with a rhythm of creation instilled by God as Creator, who rested on the seventh day. One could surmise, even eventually argue, that a *logic of sanctification* was made available for this gathered community's liturgical reasoning, beyond the human agency of Orthodox Jewish observance and any Christian presuppositions of liturgical sovereignty in a multipurpose space. At the very least, the blessing—sung in Hebrew over a cup filled with the "fruit of the vine," with all the remaining (and precise) halakic elements surrounding it observed by an Orthodox rabbi (and his Christian companion)—*set apart* the space, the time, and those gathered, many of whom testified to the space/acts *made sacred*, with holy awe. Therefore, some *logic of sanctification*

---

6. Rabbi Brad Hirschfield, personal conversation May 23, 2010. *Rosh Hashana*, Chapter 2, Mishnah 8 (Lev 1:23): Gamaliel II notes the community's role in the creation/observance of the festival calendar, as distinct from the sanctity/observance of Shabbat.

overflowed into this otherwise "non-observant" space, enacted at the very least by an Orthodox rabbi in a multipurpose room. But how is an event of liturgical reasoning like this understandable for Reformed theological Christians? Was any Reformed particularity maintained?

CHRISTIAN SACRAMENT AND "SACRAMENTAL"

First of all, Reformed Presbyterian Christians would confess no Sacrament of Communion within the events described. According to the Presbyterian constitution, specifically the Directory for Worship—the closest textual analogue in Presbyterian practice to Jewish halakah—the sacraments of Baptism and the Lord's Supper are instituted by God and commended by Christ as signs of the real presence and power of Christ in the church, symbols of God's action. Through these actions, God seals believers in redemption, renews their identity as the people of God, and marks them for service (W-1.3033; W-3.3601). The Lord's Supper is also the sign and seal of eating and drinking in communion with the crucified and risen Lord (W-2.4000). The invitation to the table is offered only for those who have been baptized, as a privilege given to the undeserving who come in faith, repentance, and love (W-2.4011).

More along the lines of halakic overview, this case did not enact the sacrament of communion: there was no invitation spoken to any table of sacrament; the table was a small one, placed in distinction from the altar table of the multipurpose space. No formal Christian liturgical language was used, especially not the Pauline "words of institution" within a Great Prayer of Thanksgiving. The bread is traditionally broken first at the altar table in a Christian Eucharist, and in this case, the bread was not liturgically broken at the table at all. No mention of Jesus was made at the table, nor was there spoken interpretation offered—Jewish or Christian. Both the Orthodox rabbi and the Presbyterian minister intuitively elected to have the actions speak for themselves—or at least be spoken through—quite distinct from any human articulation or proclamation.

On the other hand, one could argue that there *was* a *sacramental* logic at play *because both positive and prohibitive actions were engaged coincident with Presbyterian doctrine and practice.* No invitation was offered, because it was not communion. The words of institution were not said, because it was not communion. All actions *were* congruent with prescribed "right administration of the sacraments." Some were positive actions, some acts were intentionally omitted or absent in respect of Presbyterian "law." One of the positive actions, in this case, was simply pouring the cup and sharing it within a context of Christian liturgy (in heritage of Reform Jewish practice).

As Presbyterian "law" surrounding the sacrament of Communion guided the liturgical event, so it could be argued as "instituted by God and commended by Christ as signs of the real presence and power of God, symbols of God's action." Actions intentionally omitted included the invitation, the words of institution, the breaking of the bread in either Jewish or Christian custom, to name a few.

Those gathered were arguably sealed in a communal practice as people of God and marked for service. The cup was presented within a larger *logic of sacrament* which enlivened the significance of a communion chalice within Reformed theological discourse.[7] The chalice—though there were two—was common, as each was filled simultaneously and both were offered to all, hence communal; as the cup was poured, it invited appearance of the kiddush cup of Shabbat table practice, with all its significations, and it spoke a sacramental logic of a communion chalice, signifying "the shed blood of Christ poured out for the world"—not because of what was spoken but because each Christian had been shaped to perceive that meaning in previous worship communities; the unfermented grape juice—in this case, kosher wine—was even "clearly identified" and served "as an alternative for those who preferred it." Furthermore, the space for the event and the two chalices were specifically arranged and presented in view of the people, as directly prescribed by the Directory for Worship (W-1.4004; W-3.3615).

At the very least, the liturgical reasoning resourced here by observant Jewish practice and specified Presbyterian "law" somehow engaged two distinct but coincident logics which then enlivened Shabbat holiness and sacramental action. Those positive acts taken, *and those acts omitted in honor of particularity*, enlivened a Jewish and a Christian awareness of a cup, filled with the "fruit of the vine," blessed and offered to all as testimony, as an act of sanctification, remembrance, event fulfillment of an obligation

---

7. "The use of a common cup expresses the communal nature of the Sacrament and reflects the consistent scriptural reference to a single cup. Pouring into the cup signifies the shed blood of Christ poured out for the world. The manner of distribution used [may vary] ... and the session is to determine what form of the fruit of the vine is to be used.... Whenever wine is used in the Lord's Supper, unfermented grape juice should always be clearly identified and served also as an alternative for those who prefer it" ("Cup," W-3.3611).

to God and all humanity. This "non-observant," analogical form of a Shabbat eve kiddush upon conclusion of Christian liturgy assumed (if unintentionally) "the character of a sacramental act," to use Rabbi Adin Steinsaltz's words; "a sort of communion, in the performance of the *mitzvah* of union of the soul, the body, the food, and the essence of holiness."[8]

In conclusion, this teaching of the Shabbat eve kiddush upon the conclusion of a formal Christian liturgy (shaped by Jewish Reform prayer service) arguably offered a logic of sanctification alongside and kept distinct from a Christian theological *logic of sacrament* (or vice versa). The cup took on the appearance of a kiddush cup and a eucharistic chalice, each as a cup filled with the "fruit of the vine," blessed and offered in thanksgiving and fulfillment of two legal traditions within irrefutably distinct religious practices. It was both connected to and distinct from Shabbat. It was connected to and distinct from the person and work of Jesus of Nazareth, whom Christians call the Christ. Deep roots in difference and the liturgical hospitality that may unfold in the flow of devotion.

---

8. Steinsaltz, "*Kiddush* Ritual," 154.

Belief amidst Nontheism and Other

Love has surrounded me my whole life, yet something *more* broke open in me when I came face to face with a big-ass Buddha in a Tibetan center that had been a Baptist church. The Buddha and the stained glass windows of crosses, crowns, and sheep speak to one another even now in that place of ex-prayer, now meditation. A friend felt the drive to explore meditation, asking my perspective, my companionship. We learned of a Tibetan Buddhist sangha fifteen minutes from my home, and Sunday morning practice sounded inviting to her. "Will you come with me?" she asked. A Christian theology professor and preacher's wife, I said, "Sure." I felt like a security blanket, completely unaware *I* was about to be stretched myself.

We walked into the meditation hall, where the Buddha confronted us both. It might as well have shouted directly at me, given how much I flinched inside. All I could hear in my head was, "What a golden calf!" For those unfamiliar with the reference, my own tradition was screaming inside me about idolatry, infidelity to the One True God, my actions being worthy of condemnation if my own scriptures were to be taken literally. All I could say aloud, though, was "Buddha sure is big here." For the next several weeks, then months, we attended Sunday morning practices together; she listened for her path into Buddhist practices, I focused on companioning and supporting her.

About this time, a book arrived in my life with the *whoosh* of book-providence. You know that strange synchronicity when you discover the book you can't seem to stop reading while it answers some question you weren't aware you were asking? *God without Being*, by Jean-Luc Marion, was like that for me. I was delectably drawn into this volume answering a question I had not been aware I was asking. *How is it possible that I was sensing God in this Buddhist sangha of Tibetan lineage, a lineage of philosophy and practice scholars would call nontheistic and folks in my earliest communities would call godless?* The longer I practiced with this community, the deeper I knew its practice and spaces were sacred, in both a Buddhist way of "disciplined practice toward an emptiness that is fullness" and in my own tradition's sense of sacred, God enfleshed and Present. At an elemental level, the title of Marion's book resolves an ongoing, centuries-long debate—if and how God exists, whether it matters. It's really important for many of us, so we should offer a respectful nod and even a moment of silence . . .

I fell in love with Marion's book because his title takes away the fight with ne'er a scuffle. *God without Being.* He proposes some kind of sacred Other who does not exist, who has no being per se, *except the force of Love, embodied in felt sense, known in an erotic phenomenon.* Something you can *sense.* His work is much more complicated than that, of course, moving metaphysics (science of "being") into a post-metaphysical and phenomenological philosophy, theology. For our purposes here, though, the text delves into a longstanding Christian tradition (resonant with Islamic, Jewish, even Hindu traditions) of looking into the many names of God, the final and most important being that of *caritas,* love. Marion is happy to give up the word *God* in some contexts entirely, calling this in philosophical drag *love without being.* This One without Being only loves, only matters in the force of love. I *love* that. Win-win. Finally, peace at the dinner table instead of angels on pinheads or disgruntled uncles. Marion describes a love that liberates in the quest for assurance, not certainty, a love so scandalous that we betray and hide from it all the time. This *love without being* is no Hallmark card sentimentality. We yearn and then resist it, seek and then hide from it, profess it then pretend it doesn't matter, invite it then fear its claim on our lives. It's more demanding than anything imaginable, even if within its force we discover everything our deepest hearts desire.

Sensing into the force of Love, I was beginning to enter into something I knew innately but could not understand, something so deep a part of me I couldn't imagine that I'd not always known about it, though I was clearly just discovering it, or it was newly finding me. Meditation practice with my friend was part of it, as was being welcomed into a community of *practice,* more than my tradition's *faith.* Unbeknownst to me, an irrepressible, numinous journey was just beginning with a direct force and flow of this Love in my life.

One of the most important truisms in Buddhism, as you may know, is that *life is impermanent*. Nothing stays the same; everything will always change; nothing will be as your mind grasps it to be. This sangha had all kinds of issues, as any human community will, but the charism that drew them together was *practice*. Meditation practice, chanting practice, teaching and learning practices, hospitality, and yes, fidelity to the lineage of tradition in which they were *practicing*. Mindfulness. Calm abiding. Deepening encounter with oneself and the interdependence of all sentient beings. For me, though, their gift was living light-heartedly into life's impermanence, into lovingkindness.

In a very basic sense, true to their lineage of practice, no one there was seeking certainty. (Being human, of course we all were.) Over time and all of a sudden, I was being shown that *certainty* was not a pathway to love. Certainty was an obstacle to something somehow more precious. In their language made my own, certainty spoke of attachment, an inability to be in the world *as it is*, a need to make the world fit with your own desires or fears. The lamas that would come to teach didn't even talk of *love*, as a matter of fact, but *lovingkindness*. It was almost as if *love didn't have a being of its own,* apart from *acts of lovingkindness*. Each of us was being drawn into more and more uncertainty, where we could discover what my own tradition sings as blessed assurance—a deepening, overwhelming sense of abiding-with. *Love without being. Lovingkindness.* In this place of no God, in a tradition of practice from the East completely uninvested in any of the stories or habits I knew, I encountered a force of lovingkindness independent of certainty, of what I knew or didn't know, known again and again in practice.

I startled at how my world changed almost overnight. I could move into uncertainty more and more easily because doing so, within the webs of relationship focused in practice, I knew a deeper and deeper assurance in the uncertainty. Rooted deeply in body, in practice, this assurance arose without will but with willingness, without achievement but in receptivity. The teacher of this sangha, Garchen Rinpoche, taught about this "river that cannot be frozen," for which "devotion is the single essential point." Deeper and deeper assurance, devotion—they were related somehow. They required living into impermanence.

If I were willing, my deepest wounds and hungers could begin to be soothed, healed, nourished by compassionate, deeply embodied women and men. If I were willing, life would get really interesting, confusing, contradictory and more. I began to sense Presence in places the holy "He" of my tradition wasn't supposed to be. A Tibetan Buddhist sangha. A sacred liturgy shared with Jews. Coffee with an atheist. A Shabbat table with strangers becoming friends. A yurt-circle of wilding women. A circle of women practicing old and new ways of awakening in their own words and the words of others. If my heart were open to it, my life was becoming peopled with deeply soulful women and men, engaged in life-giving service of those around them, of the larger world. I was about to realize, awaken to, encounters with some of the most mindful, awakened, tenacious, and courageous people in my local contexts, and far afield as well. Here in a Buddhist ex-Baptist sanctuary, I was being drawn into more and more uncertainty with a deepening, overwhelming sense of assurance. Blessed assurance, found with non- and no-theists.

A Companionable Way

How might your life have been different
    if the love that held you could also hold the love of "other"
        without fear, will, or judgment . . .

    if there had been a place for you where
        you were welcome without obligation,
        where no one had to defend anything or
            protect anyone in order to belong . . .

    if it were a place of *assurance* more than certainty,
        trust more than belief,
            wonder more than information?

                How might your life have been different?
                How might our world be different?

Path of Conscious Love

How have I come to understand this river of devotion, this lovingkindness embedded in impermanence that offers more blessed assurance than I had ever known before? Each companionship came to life in a fashion and with a rhythm I began to recognize over time. There was a sense of a pattern but also unique expression determined by the individuals involved. *Spiritual friendship* and *anam cara* were the first descriptive terms for me to understand what began in my life there in New Jersey. "Conjugal spirituality" and the "primacy of mutual love" weren't far behind after I got married. A poignant observation arose here: it might lack breadth and depth for Christian traditions to look mainly to monastic celibates to conceive contemplation or spirituality for all, particularly as monastics have been only a small portion of the population. *Conjugal spirituality* aimed to recraft a sacred path within relationship in a holistic and more bodily expressive fashion. "Erotic celibacy"[1] was the next receiving to understand the flow of devotion experienced in the body amidst a web of covenantal relationships. Devotion can be unruly, particularly as it weaves in and out of other commitments. Lisa Isherwood explores the power of eros when welcomed and relinquished at the same time, deepening faith and transforming lives. In each of these terms, I received a way to hold the sensations and overwhelm of devotion while staying close to who I was as a fledgling church leader and then within ongoing covenantal commitments.

It was Cynthia Bourgeault's work, however, that provided the comprehensive framework I had been seeking. Beginning in an early memoiresque volume, *Love Is Stronger than Death*, she charts a pathway to spiritual transformation within intimate relationship, most recently described as the *path of conscious love*. The phrase comes from the work of John Welwood,

---

1. Isherwood, *Power of Erotic Celibacy*, 123–24.

Journey of the Heart, which takes a more therapeutic, psychological-spiritual angle on the journey. Both Bourgeault and Welwood use it to describe the force and contours of intimate relationship as spiritual practice, which is also the heart of the companionable way. Everything that follows here depends heavily upon their writings, their experience, as translated now into my own.

RELATIONSHIP AS WISDOM PRACTICE

Bourgeault's own story, her integration of it within Christian and esoteric traditions, offered a map of my Buddhist lama's phrase, the *river of devotion*. Her life and writings tendered an invitation to immerse oneself into relationship as spiritual practice. Her story about this began in a foundational relationship with a now deceased Benedictine monk named Rafe, with whom she remains in living covenant in what they call the "body of hope."[2] She charts the contours of their relationship, guided by the spiritual wisdom each had received by the time they met.

My experience is recognizable in hers, but also markedly different. Both Bourgeault and Welwood focus their work on a more traditional monogamous pairing of a man and a woman, with a hue of sexual/romantic love. The web of spiritual friendships I came to know, however, brought an intensity of connection within the body's sensuality but not within explicitly sexual relations of any kind. Companionships can uphold the same dynamics and themes as she describes, in their various ways. Each has flowed in mutually determined, bounded intimacies of deep listening and psychic relatedness, rooted by and in our multiple communities of practice. I recognized the deepening of closeness and psyche-soul connection through spiritual practice. At different times, the intensity of shadow work unfolded—the unexpected differences and conflicts to be received and navigated toward mutual understanding and growth in each of us. I began to learn a companionable way as an invitation to this web of spiritual friendships—bounded, distinct, differing levels of challenge, rooted by multiple communities of practice. Eventually, I came to recognize the same pattern, this path of conscious love, within communities that gathered in a circle way, an archetypal form of human community structured by a circle.

---

2. Bourgeault, *Love Is Stronger than Death*, 87–90.

Path of Conscious Love
Passion without Fixation

John Welwood's work offers a good introduction to the energy and force within relationship as spiritual practice. I had not known the Buddhist wisdom of devotion as fuel for the spiritual path. Welwood's description of *passion* offers what I came to know then, both in its felt-danger to my life's commitments and its accuracy in naming the gift of experience. The felt sense of this energy and force in your body can offer the best and worst of human being in committed relationship. Its fires can warm and sustain you in what you love the most—your partner, creative endeavors, vision for gifts in the world. Its fires can also consume or destroy a person. If not tended consciously and with great care, it can mislead and even threaten family relationships and friendships. The abundance and vibrancy of life I was receiving within its flow simply defied words, most of the time. It was like falling in love again and again, though completely celibate and bounded. Warming fires, then, and a mystery of sacred work with deep feeling and a sense of purpose. But it's so easy to see how the fires can overwhelm a person, making him or her question what it all means, how the connections can be healthy, bounded, and sacred. This sacred fire can destroy, in other words—spouses who cannot understand it, families who feel threatened by it, friends who see but cannot remain close within it. Companions in faith can begin to find the balance required to both grow and stay connected to their lives and loves, however, when held in diverse and larger communities of practice. Held with care, each may listen deeply and find sacred, bounded connection across difference.

Welwood charts *passion* in some of these ways, helping flesh it out a bit. He notes the spark of excitement felt when standing on the edge of the unknown, whether that be a new relationship, an adventure, or a creative work. "Two different worlds rub up against each other . . . self and other, inner and outer, familiar patterns and uncharted possibilities." The natural gift of passion is to connect intensely, to offer those willing to feel it "an intense quality of *energized presence* that puts us in touch with the fullness and richness of being alive."[3] This force attracts us to "the new," whatever that may be. As we are pulled out of our usual, however, out of the habitual patterns that create a safe and predictable life, this force can also unground us, disorient us, disrupting what we thought we knew. The way to safely ground it, he advises, is to always hold it within an I-Thou relation. Its flow

---

3. Welwood, *Journey of the Heart*, 58–59.

guides safely when we recognize that the *source* of the passion is not the object or person in our attention but a vaster sense of being that is pulling us forward, out of our habitual patterns. If we overemphasize the object or person who seems to bring us such intense energy, then passion fuels attachment and ultimately severs us from the Source of life.

Each companionship in my own journey brought this energized presence, a sense of invitation to the Holy more expansive and wondrous than I had ever imagined. I delved into various spiritual practices significant to my friends, learning "from the inside" the spiritual fire available within disciplined observance. Each invitation that arose—calm abiding meditation within my local sangha, *kashrut* observance in conversation with Jewish companions of various streams of tradition, Friday prayers with the local mosque—broke habitual patterns of seeing and receiving in me, opening me to a vaster sense of being. Each companion offered a personal window into mystery, grounded in their own lives, by their own community of practice. Of course, there were times when one of us would get distracted by the other, drawn into the sense of Presence made available by this "other." Each time, balance returned when attention was brought back to the sense of Source, the Holy named in his/her own tradition. This was—and is—delightful, though often overwhelming in institutional structures that may feel boring and irrelevant. But it's just this tried-and-true ground of institutional structure that can solidify and rebalance companions in the flow of devotion.

The invitation, the challenge named in religious traditions for centuries, is to bring the two sides together. Focusing upon Thou, holding our beloved loosely, lightly, leads to what Welwood calls "passion without fixation," or *devotion*.[4] Here, we are led to the role of conscious intention, what makes the path of conscious love viable, recognizable. You can choose to open your heart, your mind, and your body to the ache of the deep feeling of connection across all reason, all difference. You can consciously choose to direct a love without expectation—or at least less and less expectation—into the world, toward strangers, friends, family members who have wounded you. This is not an act of will, like forgiving someone who has wounded you "because that's what religious people do." No. True forgiveness requires repentance and change of heart. Devotion requires an abundance of grounded, sacred presence known deep within. But if and when you *do* choose, all the passion you feel can ripen into something deeper,

---

4. Ibid., 65.

what Welwood calls "wholehearted devotion." *This* is the powerful transformative energy "that can work magic on a human soul."[5] This is precisely the phenomenon I was experiencing, that I was searching high and low to understand in words, though my body and life knew it intimately inside. Whole-heartedness.[6] Harnessed energy for spiritual transformation. Abundance, fullness, richness of deeper being, made newly available to share open-heartedly with others. The stunning thing for me here was being directed to look inwardly for this richness, if held freely in webs of outer, life-giving relationship.

Welcoming the Disorder of Awakening

While the fruit of the journey cannot be denied—passion, richness of deeper being, energized presence, sense of being fully alive—the intensity and depth of felt-disorder can be overwhelming too, especially in aging or dying institutions seemingly incapable of receiving or stewarding such energies. Passion and the human propensity to grasp it can fuel the journey into disillusionment, vulnerability, fear—all of which serve to "break the heart open,"[7] in Welwood's words. These can foment fear, conflict, and rupture within a person or in relationships rigidly held. Conflict as opportunity for growth sounds so productive on paper, but the felt sense of it can be so destabilizing.

For instance, this path may push you into seeing parts of yourself you would rather not. Seeing more clearly who you are in the sacred gaze of another dismembers your egoic sense of self, the outer sense you want the world to see. Instead, you see more clearly who and how you are—both the fears and needs you attempt to hide *and* the strengths and gifts left unclaimed. Both can destabilize an egoic sense of self. Or you may be pushed into your earliest sensations, awakening you anew to the conditioned patterns of your youth, the version of abandonment or engulfment (or both) you experienced when you were too young to have any sense of agency to do anything about it. These "obstacles of the path" can be painful, but they break open your worldview, your expectations, your *heart*—actually the shell you've constructed around your heart to protect it.[8] Only in this

---

5. Ibid.
6. Brown, "The Power of Vulnerability."
7. Welwood, *Journey of the Heart*, 78.
8. Ibid., 79.

deeper seeing will you stretch or be stretched toward a larger vision, a more expansive encounter with the world. This brings both more wholeness, joy, *and* more difficulty, sorrow, whether your own or that of another in empathic connection. Only in this fashion does the interconnectedness of the world become visible, sensed, *known* at any depth. Only in this fashion does passion without fixation, *devotion*, become a path, a sacred way of the heart.

NUTS AND BOLTS OF A PATH OF CONSCIOUS LOVE

Bourgeault's approach to this *path of conscious love*—what she builds on esoteric traditions to call a "Fifth Way" path of wisdom—fed a deep hunger in me for language to assure my mind I was not going crazy as I met companion after companion in the flow of devotion. The elements of "intimate relationship as spiritual practice"—*kenosis, abundance, singleness*—and the overarching themes of it—*conscious work* and *shadow work*—give necessary relief for anyone in search of a pattern, an order to the nonlinear, holy and life-giving path that devotion invites in conscious love, lovingkindness, love without being.

Bourgeault describes this way of the heart as an "integrated spiritual method," both intimately familiar and radically strange for most Christians today, reared on a dualistic, largely disembodied spirituality.[9] She offers the first inklings of it in *Love Is Stronger than Death*, organized by her own narrative in the shape of a compass rose with each direction a particular spiritual lesson: "the law of last year's language," "the absence of God is the presence of God," "everything that can be had in a hug is right here," and "trust the invincibility of your own heart."[10] Stories and reflections give contour to the spiritual wisdom she learned in relationship with Rafe, who lived into the truths of *detachment, consent, inner seeing*, and *surrender*.[11] Portions of these lessons can be found in her other works as well. Leaning first into her own experience, then trusting the invincibility of her own heart in covenant with Rafe in the body of hope, Bourgeault moves this intuition and her conceptual argument into the choppy waters of Christian tradition, Mary Magdalene, and (eventually) the Holy Trinity.[12]

---

9. Bourgeault, *Meaning of Mary Magdalene*, 101.
10. Bourgeault, *Love Is Stronger than Death*, 49–75.
11. Ibid., 76.
12. Bourgeault, *Holy Trinity*, 132–53.

Speaking in Christian vernacular with a Zen twist, she prefaces her description of the path of conscious love with the invitation to return to beginner's mind, to truly be willing to see anew that about which you are already utterly convinced. Crafting Jesus as a wisdom teacher, she notes he requires "beginner's mind" or "a willingness to unlearn what one already presumably knows and start with a clean slate."[13] Within this willingness, then, three elements shape a path of conscious love as Bourgeault has experienced it with Rafe, and as she suggests lived within a companionship between Jesus and Mary Magdalene: *kenosis, abundance,* and *singleness* (unity).

Here I demur from all speculation about Mary Magdalene—historical, exegetical, pop cultural, and more—to point simply to the relational pattern I recognized in my own companionable journey. It is the pattern that is the point here. It matters little to me when historians argue for or against this relational wisdom being birthed by Mary Magdalene and Jesus, in other words. I simply name my gratitude that the wisdom tradition Bourgeault suggests and carries forward found me when it did. I recognize that about which she writes, if within the more expansive frame of spiritual friendships and circle-way communities of practice.

Kenosis and the Transfiguration of Desire

The first element, *kenosis*, refers to the emptying of oneself, the willingness "to let things come and go without grabbing on."[14] Bourgeault describes it in terms of a "warm spaciousness," a making space for something or someone else to be, to grow. "Its flow is positive and fundamentally creative," she concludes, though its intensity is counter-cultural and can be disruptive. We have few communal spaces in which emotional intelligence and spiritual maturity are described well. We live in a culture of acquisition and immediate gratification, which undermine the authentic self-emptying that counterintuitively or indirectly leads to fullness and connection. More common is the habit of mind of willing oneself to empty, or of viewing self-emptying as an act of disempowerment, self-sacrifice, even self-abnegation that we hope others will do first. Neither of those describes this movement of the soul in a vulnerable, spiritual friendship.

---

13. Bourgeault, *Meaning of Mary Magdalene*, 102.
14. Ibid., 104.

Kenosis almost cannot be intended or willed, therefore I cannot tell you *how* to do this. One self cannot tell another self to empty or how to empty without getting mired in damaging power relations shaped by consumerist habits of mind. And yet, to feel the passion and yearning of eros—what Bourgeault nicely describes as "that messy, covetous, passion-ridden quicksilver of all creation"—and do the work of nonattachment and nonaversion? You find yourself in the root energy of human being, welcomed into participation in some of life's deepest mysteries. There is a freedom of "not being in charge," of being deeply connected to your essential Self while also in the Flow of something else directing how to offer what you have.

Bourgeault names the "great secret of erotic love," which is that "*agape is in essence transfigured desire.*" In order to participate in and even "tradition" the agape love at the heart of my own Christian tradition, for instance, requires the welcoming of desire at the same time it is relinquished. Bourgeault even sets it up in an equation of sorts: $A = E \times K$: "The greater the degree of Eros present and the stronger the practice of *kenosis*, the greater is the magnitude of transfigured love thereby revealed."[15] The desire to be with your spiritual friend, then, when allowed and deeply felt, opens your heart and mind with the flow of creative energy, strong yearning. At the same time, the willingness to "hold it loosely" or to sustain the ache of separation while you live into your own life of discipleship actually deepens the connection, allows more of you to receive new awareness and *see with the heart*. Kenosis is the pillar of this pathway, made pregnant with possibilities literally unimaginable within most popular or overculture expressions.

This tension is in great contrast to how many Christian traditions conceive of love and deep feeling. Centuries of monastic discipline have been built solely on the notion of renunciation, the suppression of erotic desire because it divides the human heart. Centuries of masculinized voices, rife with dualistic-Pauline overtones, proclaim a split and the purity of spirit over the "things of the flesh." Given masculine development, meaning the developmental need to differentiate and fully separate from the mother if one is to mature as a man, this makes sense. But does the Force that creates from nothing, that can unify all things, that reconciles wounded hearts—does this Force really divide the human heart? Bourgeault faces this head on, and uses some philosophically nuanced language to say no. In her experience and interpretation of Christian traditions, Love is "in

---

15. Ibid., 121.

face the sole force strong enough to *unite* it."[16] What divides are the fixated passions and shadow, grasping side of human being, which are not "grounds for renunciation" but rather "grounds for purification." These dynamics are the stuff of soul-work, the dross to be refined and purified, not repressed and neglected.[17] God as subject of love, origin, Root, and Force of Life courses through a body willing to receive all that arises—gold and dross—for the sake of transfiguration, for another, for the awakening to the heart of both (or all) welcomed into One. The invitation is to enter fully into the yearning, the desire, knowing that the kenotic relinquishment of it offers a wholehearted devotion and awareness of interdependence previously unimaginable.

Abundance in Face of Scarcity

The second pillar of the path of conscious love, *abundance*, names the desired experience of the Holy sought by so many as the only experience of the Holy. Bourgeault calls this "a direct gateway into a divine reality that can be *immediately experienced* as both compassionate and infinitely generous."[18] This part of the path broke open my own heart, my own inner seeing, because I had been deeply immersed in mainline Protestant religious communities for most of my life. The unexpected, uncanny compassion and generosity that poured into my world from new friends and their spiritual traditions startled me out of the scarcity mentality in which I had been shaped in declining and grieving congregations. Communities of deep affection and support in my institutional service continue to grieve the loss of cultural centrality and of the public voice of Christianity. They face the exodus of their children from their towns (due to lack of opportunity) and from treasured traditions. Finding myself immersed in spiritual friendships across communities, however, an awareness of overwhelming abundance grew until all I could see was abundance. It overflowed me, my life, my language, so much so I couldn't help sharing it outwardly.

It's hard work to be a spokeswoman for abundance in a scarcity culture, however, particularly when the reigning discourse is rife with clear examples of scarcity and decline. It's not unlike being a Tigger in a roomful of Eeyores and Rabbits—all bounce and energy amidst melancholy and

16. Ibid., 92.
17. Ibid.
18. Ibid., 104.

dignified disdain. One can only point to the lens of perception and the consistency of spiritual wisdom across traditions that encourage Rafe's lessons named above: detachment, consent, inner seeing, and surrender. This abundance is all around, available to us always, though our habitual self-protections often prevent us from seeing it. Constrictive motions—what Bourgeault names taking, defending, hoarding, clinging, etc.—result in spiritual blindness. Letting go, surrender, and receptivity all open an inner seeing that "restores the broken link with the dynamic ground of reality."[19] While there is radical poverty and suffering in the world, there is also overwhelming abundance. Which do we choose to see first? It is counterintuitive that letting go is actually the doorway into the stream of abundance. This is probably what made me trust it.

Singleness—Receptive Seeing from Oneness, Wholeness

The third pillar in the path of conscious love, *singleness*, is both a habit of mind and fruit of the previous two movements of soul, kenosis and abundance. By means of self-emptying (kenosis) and the receptivity of abundance—the restored link to the dynamic ground of divine reality—the accustomed habits of mind, driven by egoic need, begin to dissolve into a single lens. "The egoic mind's compulsive need to divide the perceptual field into paired opposites" is broken open. Instead of these polarized pairs, consciousness aligns with its source and looks at the world through a oneness previously unimagined within the mind. Bourgeault describes it with reference to a Nag Hammadi text: "To be able to 'make two become one' in this fashion is to reunite with the creative principle of the universe itself."[20] In emptiness is fullness, in singleness is wholeness, unity, Oneness rooted deeply in the body by means of the heart, this *way of the heart*. Singleness, in some contrast to the traditional translation of *celibacy*, names the intimate wholeness and knowing within interdependence. "To experience abundance," says Bourgeault, "is essentially to see from oneness. . . . This gift can only be received in a state of deep inner emptiness, for any grasping and self-assertion will shatter the unity of which abundance is the mirror."

Regardless of how one receives or refuses Bourgeault's argument about Jesus's "integrated spiritual method" and its potential (or implausibility) for

19. Ibid., 105.
20. Ibid., 106.

offering Mary Magdalene a renewed and renewing position at "the heart of Christianity," this *path of conscious love* stands higher and higher in a world whose hungers are growing deeper and deeper for the very fullness and unity it suggests. Resourced within multiple traditions, it is arguably a most inclusive spiritual path. Its relationship to human embodiment is not one of dialectic or division but of integration and purification. Of course, at least in the reigning Christian traditions I know, we have few practices that conceive of embodiment as revelatory or sacred, which makes the path of conscious love hard to even perceive. This journey of companionship suggests to me that the oneness resulting from this partnership practice can arrive unexpectedly in a gathering of human beings in shared intention, spiritual friendship, and ultimately circle-way belonging, attentive to both conscious and shadow work.

Conscious and Shadow—Stewarding the Gifts of Both Light and Dark

Conscious work undergirds the entire path, which means "the first requirement of conscious love is, of course, that it has to be *conscious*—or in other words, anchored in a quality of our presence deeper than simply egoic selfhood."[21] It requires a stable inner observer or witnessing presence, knowing yourself underneath and beyond the egoic needs of protection, achievement, performance. This work invites being seen just as you are and held by your companion or the circle without judgment, with presence. Schnarch's work describes this as the self-differentiation-in-relationship required for true intimacy. In Bourgeault's words, this is "the art of separation [that] is essential to conscious love."[22] One has to stand on one's own, offer the gifts and challenges within oneself, *and* commit to doing so in a conscious balance of me/we, inner/outer desires.

This can be harder than you'd think, at the start. When you encounter someone with whom you feel a natural affinity, someone who might be a potential companion, the force of feeling that brings you together has a particular character or flavor. You find yourself with an immediate trust and an intuitive recognition of this person. There is a sense of safety and invitation that surrounds you both. The first time I met a rabbinic friend from out of town, we finished each other's sentences, somehow attuned to

21. Ibid., 118.
22. Ibid., 119.

the river of devotion that had opened between us. We knew a yearning to be in conversation, to teach and learn with one another. There is often a strong sense that it is safe to hold nothing back.

Naturally, *shadow work* unfolds then, fired by devotion into conscious awareness, driving the self- and other-transfiguration. Bourgeault describes the egoic selves we construct as the "soul cages" meant to protect our most tender places. An ego-centered self-image allows us to move freely in the world without constant threat of vulnerability or pain. When companions find one another, there is a welcome open-door feeling. A dance begins, between their deepest yearnings and their strongest held fears. Bourgeault calls it "the approach-avoidance dance" that sets companions on "an inevitable collision course."[23] The deepest yearnings keep drawing companions back to the sacred fire between them; the fears and realities of who each really is, seen and mirrored so clearly one by the other, painfully refine each in that sacred fire. Held with honesty, trust, a huge amount of inner witnessing and the mysterious Force of Love itself, however, companions may finally set each other free.[24] This is a steady and tumultuous path of self-confrontation—as each is willing, of course—held gently in a tenacious love. "Shadow work" describes this terrifying but ultimately freeing self-transformation in which gifts that have been unclaimed and limitations that have been neglected come into a holy light. It is a self-transfiguring process of moving more and more deeply into the infinite invitation of divine-human Self-discovery within relationship as spiritual practice.

Sense of Interdependence—*Body of Hope*

One of the most powerful motivations I find for exploring the path of conscious love is the palpable sense of interdependence that arises, even if just a moment from time to time. Bourgeault observes that with patience and practice, companions find themselves in "one body," or an abiding state of being in which all the warring factions of their being(s) lead to an inner sense of wholeness, "singleness," integrity. This is not the narrowed sense of *henosis* or "one-fleshness" named within understandings of marriage[25] so much as it is energetic belonging in the web of creation, a felt sense of being interdependent with everything around and within you. When you

---

23. Ibid., 123.
24. Ibid.
25. Oliver, *Conjugal Spirituality*, 42–54.

have repeated moments of this awareness, this felt sense, it becomes harder and harder to see "others" as apart, as "other-ized" in our culture. Each person certainly retains his/her own complete otherness, mystery, incomprehensibility, wonder. But the open-heart or heart-seeing way of encounter, in what Bourgeault calls "the alchemy of love," creates a felt sense of connection, even in disagreement or disconnection. This sense of "body" or "state of being" is known as the "body of hope" in Bourgeault's terms. She uses *energy*, *tincture*, and *conscious will* to describe this body, relying upon highly esoteric wisdom traditions to name her experience.[26] I do not want to distract from this description of relationship as spiritual practice, but it does seem important to name the sensate awareness of what she describes. My own language for it is simply a sense of interdependence, oneness, even an "intimacy of difference."[27]

There is palpable sensation to interdependence, at least as I've been given to receive it. Your experience may very well differ dramatically. *Energy* names the "raw infusion of vitality" that arrives in your system when you're consciously connected to the body of hope. "There is that immediate infusion of energy, and with it a strange sense of initiation—of being connected to one's real identity and destination. And there is that profound, encircling experience of love that brings its own certainty."[28] The sensation of this brings both deep joy and sorrow too—vitality of an overwhelming web of belonging *and* the sense of pain shared by so many. Tincture and conscious will bring a particularity into the picture. Tincture describes a quality of aliveness that has its own signature, that is unique to the physical carrier of that life. Bourgeault describes it as "a recognition of things by their inner spiritual scent." Having shared in this path with Rafe for years, she can recognize his energy, in other words. It takes practice to awaken to this quality of aliveness, but it names the melding of energies in interdependence unlike anything in our worlds of perceived separation. Conscious will, for Bourgeault, then names the experience of "an ongoing will, capable of lively and pointed interaction" available in this body of hope—what I call a web of interdependence. In the highly divided, polarized habits of our world today, one has to consciously choose to awaken again and again to this unseen but available world all around us.

---

26. Bourgeault, *Love Is Stronger than Death*, 87–97.
27. Hess, "Toward an *Intimacy of Difference*," 97–114.
28. Ibid., 92–93.

CONCLUSION

Much of this path of conscious love can seem esoteric, even highly abstracted from the concrete tasks and experiences of life in religious or political or educational communities today. Yet I bow to Bourgeault's (and Welwood's) work, appreciative of its contribution to my own understanding and conceptual articulation of what these nearly twenty years have offered. There is a lot about this pattern or pathway I will never pretend to understand. But this *path of conscious love* describes almost perfectly the dynamics and contour of my own companionable journey in the river of devotion, its pathway into companionship after companionship. There is excruciating beauty in the kenosis, abundance, and unity of such relationships. Each has required a deepening of conscious work and the shadow work necessary to engage the core of who I am and have become within spiritual friendships, more broadly within circle communities of practice.

Fidelity in the Fear of Betrayal

I was running scared at the beginning of my first job at a church in New Jersey. The energy in my body had grown by leaps and bounds, which made running—even several miles a week—seem like a good outlet. I knew not why I felt so overwhelmed, nor did I know how to steward it in any other way. I had begun learning meditation with a friend exploring Buddhist meditation herself. I was learning to sit within my own skin, discovering an inner observer somewhat new to the rest of me living outwardly in the world. But deep feeling body-wisdom is not a charism of my family, immediate or extended. Though a deeply sensate capacity awoke in me when I was about six or seven, my heritage is Pennsylvania Deutsch, German-American background. We categorize and conceptualize feelings. We don't feel them, for heaven's sake, let alone trust them. I had hidden most sensate-awareness within me deep inside, ashamed of it from an early age. Perhaps it was nearing time to find words for what I feared, I thought to myself.

"Laura" and I had become quite close fairly quickly. I felt fear of her even as I felt an ease with her. Better that I let her know something was happening with me that I did not understand, so she could keep her distance. I didn't want to betray our fledgling friendship or overwhelm it with the darkness I felt and feared inside. So she and I set a time on the phone to meet at her house the next morning. Her husband had the flu. "Let's meet at the grotto close to the bay," she said. I put the *anam cara* ring on my right index finger as an intention to keep grounded in my life as it was, with my boyfriend, a gentling literate soul, within a teaching/learning life we valued. I would not betray myself or anyone I loved. Laura's car was there in the parking lot when I arrived. She got out as I did, and we walked through the arbor together. For a time, we sat on a bench, in the gaze of the Marian figure.

"I'm not sure how to begin," I began. "At the very least, I cannot bathe as sacred that which is not." Her eyes softened. She smiled. "I was thinking about you the other day," she said. "I realized something remarkable." An impish tone entered into her voice, a gentle strength with expansive warmth. "It feels like we're married somehow, in a covenant of some kind. Is not that wonderful?" She touched my hand, gently, covering it with her own.

All of me felt it at once—a sensate warmth in my chest, a tectonic shift in my belly, an expansiveness beyond anything I'd ever known. Early childhood returned. There was no Shame in awakening. None. My eyes met hers in a gentle gaze, lingering there, amazed there was no disdain or fear in her. I gazed at her for a long time, waiting for condemnation, accusation, of . . . I didn't know. For what? I'm not sure. Spaciousness opened. A light holy breath rushed into every dark space I had known. Even if it were to be for just that moment, I realized I would know for the rest of my life: the old, dusty language of my parents' religion had a *feeling*. Sanctification *could be sensed*. When honored in her eyes, in the touch of her hand, my shame-ridden body was transfigured in a sensate love that overpowered my fear.

We sat for a time, held within a Force of Love we neither expected nor knew precisely how to hold. I remember the breeze, the sound of the bubbling fountain. The autumn air with a touch of crispness to it. "I should get back to the retreat center," I finally said, softly. "Yes," she smiled. We stood, embraced a short while, then walked back to our cars.

When I arrived home the next day, my boyfriend and I sat on the couches downstairs, getting ready to watch a movie. I told him I'd had an unusual day that I didn't quite know what to do with. "Yes?" he smiled. His smile flattened a little with the weight of my words, unsure of what was unfolding within me and how it might impact him. I told him about the previous morning, my fears, and Laura's startling ability to release them in a healing touch. I named the mutual commitment of spiritual friendship that arose with her and spoke of my inability to suppress what I felt so deeply. More than that—I sense I was being called to let the friendship develop. At some intuitive level, I knew what was growing in me, in us, was not about sex or sexual gratification, which could have been easy to accomplish, had Laura and I desired it. "It's not about sex or sexuality," I told him. "Something else so deeply healing and sanctifying is happening. Laura knows it too." Yes, I was so very drawn to her but also to myself, to him, to *life*.

Fidelity in the Fear of Betrayal

It was a tough conversation for any couple, let alone two people so committed to theological education, exacerbated by ideological politics about ordination standards. If it weren't for the strength of this man, his own tenacious hold on himself and his love for me, I wouldn't be who I am today. Without my own strength, tenacious hold on myself and my love for him, he wouldn't be who he is today either. Neither of us knew what opening to an unexpected energetic force in me would mean for us. These decades later, after fifteen years of marriage, we both know the sacred calling this pathway became.

But back then, two women of faith held themselves with care while being held in an overwhelming Presence. They received the gift of their own bodies' holiness, a language and embodied-chaste Word neither could have known without the other. Had I not been formally trained in Christian traditions, with a strengthening professional identity, I could easily have interpreted this as a crisis of sexual orientation. Had it not been for Jesus and the logic of Incarnation, had it not been for the Marian figure and a grotto holding our spoken, sacred intention in Presence, I would not have withstood these incongruities nor the imposition of interpretive categories by the church and culture, particularly as these interpretive categories engender fear and self-loathing that is internalized then projected. "Church," as it is often configured today, holds less and less safety and hospitality for a risked life of faith overflowing its polarized categories and patriarchal structures.

Understanding and receiving these gifts of abundance—as well as the pain, fear, doubt—opened the doorway to feel connected, devoted, to Laura, seemingly without effort. The wellspring of deep feeling opened in both of us, allowing each to see the other with eyes of compassion and invitation, mirroring gifts the other had but could not yet claim. Being seen by her in this way planted seeds of belief and confidence I had never known. Seeing her in this way spurred in me such fierce, gentle fire for her best self, her well-being alongside her husband and family, no matter what. She felt it too. She was the one to call me out as the poet I am, though I had not remembered nor imagined that to be so since the ninth grade, when a teacher had deeply wounded my creative self. "You do know you're a poet, don't you?" she wrote as a "throwaway line" in an evening e-mail. Four hours later, 3 a.m., my first poem as an adult was born.

> Seeing and being seen
> No more than a guessed

> response to the Host.
> How do we know
> who sees best (among the three)
> the truths that awaken us, that
> illuminate both night and fear,
> faith beyond bounds, invitation clear?
> Spirit struggles for word, to name, to know
> The baptism tears
> Two worlds coming to One.

This abundance of devotion has now flowed over my life to every companion who has joined me since that day in the New Jersey grotto ... each soul-friend who is Buddhist, Jewish, pagan, differently Christian, "none," feminist, earth-spirituality centered, seeking, and more. These are the ones, the One, who create(s) my soul-life today, and they *are* many, even as they are of One.

It had been a season of running sacred, as it turns out. To receive the deep feeling of which I am capable touched a deep scar from an early age, reared in a family heritage unable to hold feeling or embodied sensation well. I had been scared because opening to this energy in my body, in my life, had felt like a betrayal of some kind, a dangerous revealing. Yet a deeper and deeper fidelity to the best of human becoming—while detached, noting consent, mirroring inner seeing, and surrendering—was born in this willingness to feel so deeply and within the body. Fidelity and healing blossomed in Laura's willingness to see me, in my willingness to see her, as we both entered into the spiritual friendship that would make us companions in spiritual practice and sacred gaze. It turns out that fidelity and fear of betrayal can be uneasy but beautiful partners in disruption that heals, brings wholeness, transforming embodied spirits.

Fidelity in the Fear of Betrayal

How might your life have been different if,
    in the beginning, there had been a place

for your own sacred beauty and deep feeling to be heard and held,
    without shame, without fear,
        welcomed with the eyes of love?

For being seen and mirrored in this love, held in darkness and light
    where *everything* could be welcomed deeply in your own body,
        attuned to the bodies around you,

where you could receive your innate giftedness,
    know your own goodness alongside limitation,
        your invitations alongside a sacred purpose?

                How might your life have been different?
                How might our world be different?

Devotion

"The river that cannot be frozen." This was a phrase I first heard from my Buddhist sangha's founding lama, Garchen Rinpoche, in a teaching on devotion. "Devotion is the single essential point," he said. "A drop of tears by the force of devotion purifies or dispels a mountain of obscurations.... The single most important source of blessings is devotion." In terms that were quite foreign to me, he was inviting into my life a curiosity and practical investigation of a force of love felt in my bones, lived in any community intent upon lovingkindness, what I will name with Jean-Luc Marion a *love without being*.[1]

This force erupts and bubbles up in every wisdom tradition I have encountered, though the practice and language around it differs widely. I first encountered it in Kagyu-Nyingma lineages of Tibetan Buddhism, but I then learned of *bhakti* in Hindi traditions. Aiming for a more contemporary, less complex term in my own work, I landed on *delight* to describe this holistic, fully enfleshed life devoted to sacred endeavor and light-hearted wisdom. I wanted a word to name a life receptive to suffering of self and other and proactive for healing and truth becoming in the world. I resisted a succinct definition, but noted delight's relationship to a capacity for wonder, not self-deception, risked trust, not certainty. It arises in compassion unexpected and hidden wounds healed.[2] Then a friend long steeped in Jewish mysticism named this force I knew as delight to be the center and drive within his own sacred journeying through kabbalah in the Tanya.[3] *Bliss* was the word he used, translation of the Hebrew. However one attempts to name this force or steward it within daily life, *devotion* seems the best fit for

---

1. Marion, *Erotic Phenomenon*, 1–10.
2. Hess, *Artisanal Theology*, 9; Hess, *Learning in a Musical Key*, 13.
3. Steinsaltz, *Opening the Tanya*, 182–83. See Zalman, *Tanya*, 104–7.

the center of a companionable way—both drive and destination, invitation and sanctuary amidst all that the world pours into us today.

In these years of running, and the spiritual companionships begun from the first church position I ever held, I began to receive a regular awareness that was sensate, embodied. It was a flow of feeling that seemed to be an intense path of transformation. Or perhaps better named transfiguration,[4] because it was reconfiguring my past and present body-awarenesses in spacious and gracious ways. Few, if any, in my Pennsylvania Deutsch family line have supple enough categories for the healing force of Life devotion offers. Body is largely a site of fear, distrust, and regulation. I *know* my own web of relationships in family and church continues to fear devotion's force, its power, its irrepressibility for transfiguration, inviting them into Spirit's intimacies. I daresay today's congregational bodies are not prepared for this deep feeling either. Contrary to these fears, however, I have learned that the rising sensation, the ebb and flow of a deep belly yearning, is not something to be denied, or shameful. Eros, as I have learned to call it, is to be a sign of wholeness, connection, and psychic relatedness[5] with others.

James Olthuis refines some of our communal habits of mind about this rising sensate-awareness, naming an ethos of mutuality and nonpossessive, noncompetitive feeling recognizable in spiritual friendships. In an essay describing "sojourning in the wild spaces of love," he distinguishes the force of eros in a helpful way. This erotic force need not be an "urge to unite" with sexual connotations, but more an urge to connect. "With the focus on *Eros* as the desire to connect, as the passion for mutuality and right relation, we have the possibility for non-possessive, non-competitive (i.e., non-violent) connecting, co-partnering, co-birthing, in the interspaces of love and creativity."[6] Much later in my own learning, but much earlier within literary history, Esther Harding's work, *Woman's Mysteries: Ancient and Modern*, names this same connection. "Eros is used in its philosophical sense, where it represents the principle of psychic relatedness. . . . The erotic is one field in which the Eros manifests itself, but not the only one."[7] Or later in the text, "The Eros is a spiritual or psychological principle, or, in the older term, it is a divinity. To be related to this principle means to be

---

4. Ross, *Writing the Icon*, xxii.
5. Harding, *Woman's Mysteries*, 29–34.
6. Olthuis, "Crossing the Threshold," 248.
7. Harding, *Woman's Mysteries*, 29 n. 1.

orientated to that which transcends personal aims and ambitions."[8] Both Olthuis and Harding open a space to receive Garchen Rinpoche's teaching on devotion. Devotion can connect us with others, but not necessarily with the sexual overtones so present in the overculture of media-blitz consumerism.

Philosopher Jean-Luc Marion names the experience with his *erotic phenomenon* in which a *love without being* grows in direct proportion to the *reduction of reciprocity* and *insufficiency of reason*.[9] Marion is writing out of a complicated philosophical tradition, challenging long-held notions in metaphysics with a return to the body, of sorts, many call *phenomenology*. For our purposes, *love without being* names the force of Love known by many names. Its substance or essence is less important. Its phenomenon beckons us all. While he might demur from the comparison, I resonated deeply with his work naming the dynamics I knew in devotion. Devotion grows when there is less and less *expectation for* return, for reciprocation. Reduction of reciprocity. It is a free gift offered into the world, rooted only in its own rationality of love-lived-in-the-cells. Not a socially defined love of provision and consumption, with designated certainty and historical vow or contract. Instead, devotion lives as an unexpectedly answered quest for assurance, a discovery that learning to love first from one's deepest Self opens—in its own time—a door to abundance and Life. *Insufficiency of reason*, as we know it today. When one lives into small attempts to love first, to love without expectation or attachment, abundance grows everywhere.

Empowered now by older voices, I have come to understand *devotion* as a yearning for connection that has its source in abundance of relationship, a real and determinative energetic web of relatedness out of which a force of love arises from so deep within that it cannot *but* be shared outwardly. It is a flow of Life that holds a bodysoul with gentling care while moving it toward growth, transfiguration, and unimaginable beauty amidst the muck and mire of the world's soils.

My language for this experience was first solely Christian, as I have steeped for nearly four decades in Christian traditions. I would name my sense of "Jesus present in the power of the Spirit" for this sacred fire, this holy yearning that drew me outward by first rooting me truly within who I am, just as I am. "Human spirit posited in the power of Spirit" also named it in formal theological terms inherited from my East Coast training and

---

8. Ibid., 33–34.
9. Marion, *Erotic Phenomenon*, 67–81.

mentored learning with James Loder. But because I was learning and receiving both within and outside my own tradition, I also strained to name it without tradition-specific language, if possible. In that vein, devotion is a generative, holistic, even holy driving force of connection that reaches outside the self toward what some scholars call "a horizon of ultimate meaning."[10] I recognized it in the energies between spiritual teachers and their students, professors and their graduate students, spiritual companions who find themselves sharing a path.

For me to receive it, truly receive it, however, took courage and a willingness to depart from my own community's norms: that is, fidelity in the fear of betrayal. I had had few, if any, categories or tools with which to make sense of the physical sensations and cognitive overwhelm *devotion* had brought into my being, into my awareness. I remember feeling ashamed, potentially guilty of some indiscretion, because this love arrived so deeply in my body, seemingly out of bounds but not. It did not grasp nor demand anything except receptivity and willingness to feel, to receive. Today, the felt sensation is welcome, familiar even. The goad to write is no longer for understanding amidst shame or fear. Devotion is a gift of Spirit, a beautiful force of Life that connects those who are different and similar in a web of compassion for all. Deeply embodied, tinged with the eros of Spirit-creation, it is a sensation and unruly overwhelm of cognition by a beautiful, potentially unnerving—actually *re*-nerving—force of Life that seems to come from elsewhere even as it is irrepressibly intimate in body. It is exquisitely, sometimes excruciatingly intimate, attracting, enlivening of body and mind, opening of heart and spirit.

DEVOTION, CHRISTIAN

This sense of the word *devotion* bears little resemblance to what the word used to mean to me, of course, particularly growing up in Midwestern America, small-town Ohio. In the rather puritanical Protestantism in which I arrived upon my birth, "devotion" was always plural and never of the body or, in the language of the time, "of the flesh." I would hear, for instance, "Have you done your devotions today?" Or "He begins every day with devotions, a sure sign of his deep faith." Devotion was something willed, a Christianized duty or obligation within which a relationship with God was pursued, even achieved "in grace." In that vein, I have been a devoted

10. Schneiders, "Study of Christian Spirituality," 17.

Christian for decades, with absolutely no preparation for the wellspring of the aforementioned devotion erupting in my own life, my own sensate experience. The history of relationship in my own life between the One called Jesus and the unruly, sensate devotion arriving into my own flesh and bones is complicated, not least by me.

Devotion to God. Devotion in Jesus. Devotion with Spirit. I struggle to write about the Holy One so many in my world know as Him, given the deep woundedness in our culture today from "cultural Christianity" or institutionalized religion. The crumbling structures of local congregations in Christian community—at least the more mainline expressions of it I know—are grieving and socialized to wield the historical Jesus as a weapon, perhaps less welcoming to a present and contemporary One. So many whom I love dearly have plentiful reasons to veer away from *anyone* who wields Jesus's name, whether it's with casual, cultural presumption or long-lived devotion. Some are women and men with earned scars of awakening in a tradition bent on dehumanizing and excluding them for who they are. Some are women and men deeply rooted in other wisdom and/or religious traditions, particularly Judaism, in which "Jesus" has been a focal point or cause of violence, even horror. Others are men and women for whom the name of Jesus symbolizes nothing but hypocrisy, preferred ignorance, an inability to engage religious faith in Him intellectually or critically.

Finding myself in the flow of devotion with such diverse companions, I have learned that sometimes my devotion *to* Jesus must rest without words, silently *in Him*, in order to be *with Him* instead of gossiping *about Him* in some injurious way. For many in my own community, this learning is deemed unfaithful, a betrayal of Jesus, rooted in a fear to stand on my own convictions and claim Jesus openly as my Lord and Savior. Maybe they're right, these brothers and sisters in Christ whose words and faith expressions hold Jesus's name in their way with such tenacity. If I hold the Name in holy quiet in order to bow to the truth of God in every "other" I meet, I must also bow to the truth of God in those who judge so. Every speaking can have its seed of truth, after all, in a world where the Spirit of God creates and redeems for good whatever we do within love's intention. Such quieted receptivity, however, invites *being-with*, *being-in*, which feels less violent than either participating in blaring the Name in contradiction to such Presence *or* denying the Name in contradiction to Whom I know in this One called Jesus.

As I said, it's complicated.

Writing about Jesus is also complicated for me because at different times, different "senses" of love have held me *in Him*. "His" felt-Presence has been fatherly, motherly, sisterly, brotherly, and friend. Over the years, "He" has pointed to a "wholly Other" Presence at the same time He then became Beloved, the One in whom an inner and outer marriage has unfolded over years. To experience each of these in my own bodysense makes talking about him difficult, as many of these loves in the body do not coexist easily. The love of a Mother, of a Brother, and the sensations of a Lover play different chords in the body, for instance. But the difficulty also resembles the startling experience of a widow attempting to remember the face of her departed husband only a year after his death. Many widows and widowers describe this awareness, being unable to recall with precision their own beloved's *face*. It startles them with a fearful, tender sense that *loss is happening all over again*. The reality, however, is that a beloved sees another beloved's face in countless facets of expression, such intimate detail over years and diverse circumstance, that remembering one perceptible face becomes impossible. By now, into the over four decades of my own Christian self-understanding, Jesus has had so many faces, Faces, that I struggle to describe my love or frustration with just one, just One.

Paradoxically, then, *Jesus* names for me both Invitation and Way of holding the conceptual "many" and the felt sense "one." Within a churched childhood and an unchurching young adulthood, I have been held both securely and loosely within His association and affection. Conceptually, I have pursued him in decades of theological formation shaping me as an established Christian insider, a recognized leader ordained to the functions of "teaching elder" in a Reformed strand of Christian tradition. That storyline could just as easily read "I have been pursued by Him in decades of theological formation, being shaped as a companion, bride of Christ, held now in bodysense and soul in scripturally rooted covenants of devotion to be discovered, received, in these more recent years." However the language arises, devotion to Jesus, in Jesus, with Jesus undergirds everything that has been said and that is yet to come. I leave it to Him that the relationship and practices in which He has led my path challenge historical, scriptural, and ecclesial senses of Him today. That's not my fault, nor is it my necessary concern.

The Jesus I know, with Whom I live into this inner-outer Marriage, comes to me in the church, outside the church, in the Presence felt with others when I relinquish His spoken name, and in the silence of listening and contemplation focused within Him in some fashion. There have been times when He has seemed my enemy, mirroring or challenging things about myself or my world I'd rather not have seen, experienced, known. But I've found He's even trustworthy in the felt-absences, which has been more often than not these last years. I lose "my Jesus" all the time, in His impermanence, having learned to trust that He will be found, again and again. Much as the Emmaus story in Luke suggests, this losing-finding reality seems unavoidable for anyone who takes wisdom-walking into resurrection life seriously. As soon as you recognize him "in the breaking of the bread" or "on the road," then He vanishes, moving ahead of you on the road to come. What is one supposed to do with a "dead man walkin'" anyway, besides learn to see anew, learn to look for Him in unusual or unexpected places? Furthermore, if the dead has arisen, if Life is ultimately stronger than death, then every apparent truth has an opposite locked within it. Every "sure thing" has a glimmer of uncertainty or possibility to be "other" than expected. In this way, it's not all that unusual for a devout, Jesus-lovin' woman, bride, to lose her Jesus again and again, only to be delighted again and again in the finding and being found.

In sum, devotion is irreparably particular though available to anyone willing to return to the body, connected with the uniqueness of human persons and our intimate and communal narratives, struggles, ways of being in the world. Devotion arises in an individual willing to open heart and mind to another whereby the Life between them becomes Real, groundless, and liberating for them both as they live it into the world around them, within their ongoing webs of social relationships unfamiliar and potentially threatened by its force. Devotion is exquisitely intimate, therefore, but free. Which does not mean without cost. It's a wisdom path that de-stabilizes as it grows, transforming all who walk it. It is freely chosen, in one sense. It is free to share and be shared, to shape and be shaped by others' mind(s) and wisdom. It also "happens" to you, with a sense of "choicelessness" too.

Garchen Rinpoche's opening words were, "You are so fortunate to have met the Dharma with devotion." I knew this. I know what he was naming. Then, I would have said "Gospel" for "Dharma" and a living sense of "Jesus" for devotion. Not to presume they are remotely the same thing but to honor my own need to find my way in familiar words amidst traditions that were not my own, would never be my own. In this way, I could receive, just as I am. And I am so very thankful. I am so very fortunate indeed. Devotion has fired my own journey of awakening. It *is* a most holy gift, as enlivening as it can be heavy to withstand, at times. "No one *wants* to want,"[11] after all, quoting David Schnarch. To yearn, to know the fullness of God—as much as one can hold, at least—necessarily means withstanding the emptiness or absence of God as well. The ego *loves* the fullness, pleasure, confirmation of itself being received by a Subject of devotion *and* it is broken open, torn asunder, as it needs to be, immersed in the utter freedom and effervescence of devotion.

Today, I welcome devotion and its teachings with the best stewardship I've been given to know, moment by moment, step by step, knowing sometimes the ache can be overwhelming, with rest found only in the One who planted the seeds of devotion in the first place. I invite any who are willing to glimpse devotion's self-emptying power, its gentling welcome into sensation and cognitive overwhelm for good. It may be heavy to carry in a world that wants nothing but light, but devotion *will* ground your own journey and nourish your own deepest hungers, again and again and again. Freely given, costly to receive, both. This devotion is a source of living water spoken about within historic religious traditions, though many now have lost the felt sense of the Life that beckons so deeply. Within traditions, beyond traditions, a river that cannot be frozen.

---

11. Schnarch, *Passionate Marriage*, 100.

Befriending Outsiders

One Saturday night in the Bronx, there was no place to be, inside or out. The May evening eased in with good conversation after a Shabbat meal. Old friends had made new friends. Children's toys had become a crunchy carpet on the living room's hardwood floors. A special evening prayer service beckoned from the local shtiebel, an ultraOrthodox Jewish prayer house. A new friend was honoring his father, of blessed memory, and everyone wanted to come. So clothes were changed, head coverings for the women were received, and two men and two women left for the service. We met another outside the door.

The shtiebel was no more than an old neighborhood home, except for a children's plastic picnic table and a bench by the neighbor's fence. Its outer ring felt like a city playground, with cracked concrete sidewalks broken by the persistence of time and play. Entering through the rickety metal door squeezed you into Eastern Europe, uncertain of return. Or whether you even wanted to be there. The door opened into a room with two or three pews, randomly scattered with old books and boxes of forgotten clothes. There were shelves with more old books on one side, a hallway into the kitchen and a bathroom on the other side. Up ahead was the gender line, a partial wall of side-boarding, half of which was horizontal plastic windows covered by a yellowing lace curtain. Windows that had begun as a barrier-less barrier had now become a veil. The women sat with the storage while the men proceeded beyond the veil. Voices of private welcome wafted over the line into the storage area. A prayer service had begun.

My ovaried compatriot and I retrieved a prayerbook from the shelf and she opened it to the appropriate section. She followed for a bit, sharing with me where we were supposed to be. Supposed to be. Something raw welled up in my throat. Where *were* we supposed to be? With the books no one read, and the hand-me-downs, left behind? I motioned to the outside, and she smiled, I think with relief. The evening air was both warm and crisp, inviting and edgy. We sat down on the neighborly-fenced bench and breathed into a silence, buffered by muffled prayers.

We mused in our separation, she as a Jewish outsider and I as a Christian one. She had long ago made her peace with such a place, such communal habits. I envied her buoyancy and spirit, seemingly unruffled by sitting with storage. I warmed immediately to her wisdom, shared openly as she shed light on her story, her loves, her family, her life. Here was a fullness to be cherished, which she did. But for me, there was no place to be. I was an outsider in nearly every respect, or so it seemed. We thought of returning to her home, where the children were being cared for by another mother in the community. My path is a childless one. Being relegated to the childcare of others was worse than sitting, unwelcome, outside a shtiebel. We looked into the shtiebel to see how far along the prayers were, but nothing was there to let us know. We returned to the plastic bench and listened as the night rolled in.

Sustaining such empty space inside me for ninety minutes was about all I could muster. The rawness in my throat got the best of me, and taking my head covering off, I stormed the shtiebel. Two men in the hallway said they thought my husband was inside and nodded their heads in his direction. I took it as invitation and stuck my head beyond the line, past the lace. A pointing to the wrist-watch, a look of impatience, and my message of impatient inquiry, desire to exist again, was received. A couple of minutes later, two men returned to the outside. One, a Jewish insider, exclaimed relief at being on the outside. "Back to the world!" he exclaimed. "Where have we *been*?" I startled to realize he, too, had felt like an outsider. The other, my husband, peered at me with fear and uncertainty. We kissed, but we both knew I had left and not returned. We left the shtiebel for the home with the toyed carpet, minus my friend's husband, minus me.

So where was I supposed to be? Where did "I" go? And more importantly, would "I" return? Amidst my friends' generous hospitality the entire weekend, I had felt part of a Modern Orthodox (Jewish) family. As a Presbyterian Christian from the Midwestern state of Ohio, no less. But there, outside the shtiebel, my body felt so very clearly what an outsider I am, will always be, in all Jewish circles. I was never supposed to be there in the first place. "My kind," meaning in this sense "Christians," perpetrated such horror on the Jews of Eastern Europe that there was literally no place for me as a Christian, let alone a woman. I was supposed to be anywhere but there. Yet there "I" was, becoming absent. Becoming present.

Where did "I" go? The first place, I now know, was into my new friend's life. While "I" had no place to be, she shared a life and story for me to be in, for a time. We spoke so easily, as women can, sharing generously of our early stories, our challenges with work and family, our hopes for adventure and ease. Both she and her husband invited me in so hospitably, I felt at home in observance and rituals I knew little about. Their devotion held me deeply, inside and out.

But still, I went to my own darkest spaces: gender imposition, choosing childlessness, suffocating religious custom. I have lived my life unconsciously crossing various gender lines, storming shtiebels of every size and shape, unaware of the cost in me as a woman to do so. *Choosing childlessness* is nearly incomprehensible in most Jewish communities into which I have been welcomed. What if more and more Jewish women chose not to have children? What would become of the Jewish community? This was yet a prayerful decision by my husband and me, confirmed again and again, if costly in misunderstanding in many circles of church and community. Last, my life is hell-bent against religion that suffocates its peripheries with pushes to center, ordained by men. My sister is a rigidly professed Christian whose relation to the world takes my breath away. I literally cannot breathe for long in her world, nor can she with me in mine. I experience her religion as exclusion, silencing orthodoxy, intentional unconsciousness of the beautiful complexity of human life as it is. But because I love my sister, I am regularly returned to this suffocating space, in an unavoidable and intimate way. Sitting at the shtiebel, "I" went to each of these places in which my mind and spirit are tender, socially outraged, potentially silenced.

Yet I did return, or was returned to myself, in the spaciousness of spirit-friendship across irreconcilable difference. The Jewish insider who exclaimed his own relief at leaving the shtiebel welcomed *me* back with a hug of return on the cracked pavement. As soon as we returned to our friends' home, I changed back into my own clothes. My friend's husband returned and when Shabbat was over, he and I jumped into the van to pick up their daughter from *her* Shabbat stay over. Spirit-friends, he and I listened together for what was beautiful and holy about a shtiebel, and about storming it, so empty for me. Hearing his awareness of emptiness, shared with me, I breathed a bit more easily. We lamented that sometimes there are simply limits across which it is too painful to reach. More breath returned.

I knew I was going to be fine as I returned slowly to my spirited skin once again. As the outsider I was, I had yet been beautifully befriended across irreconcilable difference.

There's great freedom in being in one's own skin, not attempting to be anyone or anywhere else. Great pain awaits there too, however, when you hit a wall of irreconcilable difference. How may we access deep spirit-connection across difference with the least pain? How do we honor each amidst the necessary and real limitation for both, all? I'm not sure there is an abstracted answer to those questions. Each of us needs to be willing, when invited, to enter into others' "worlds" and learn how to deeply befriend others that come into "ours." I did learn one thing without doubt: I was an outsider befriended, held in a deepening devotion of spirit-friendship, *and* I cannot and will not sit *silently* with storage.

A Companionable Way

How might your life have been different if . . .
    who you are—just as you are—
        opened doors to the Sacred within *and* beyond you
            crafted your welcome without question or obligation
                without translation or accommodation to the fears of others?

If . . .
    . . . you had a place where you were seen,
        held in all darkness and light
    . . . you knew a place where everything that arises in you—
        curiosity, sadness, wonder, fear,
            happiness, anger, loneliness, jealousy, rage—
    . . . *everything* could be welcomed deeply
        sensed as *welcome* in your own body,
            attuned to the bodies around you . . .

                How might your life have been different?
                How might our world be different?

Seeing With the Heart

Part of the reason that devotion overwhelms and disrupts, often with fear and aversion, arises from the manner in which we conceive of *knowledge* today. And *love*, for that matter. James Olthuis gathered several voices on the frontier of philosophy and spirituality to reflect on *knowing other-wise*, with an "ear of compassion and an eye of love." They write to contrast many of our contemporary assumptions about knowledge. Their work resists knowledge as objective information, rooted in a universal reason, able to be shared freely between "reasonable" people. Think of a contemporary form of expertise, for example. What commentators do we bring into our media studios, to give us "knowledge" about something? They are credentialed, often from institutions long steeped in technological habits of mind, with dispassionate, "cool-reason" approaches to whatever the subject matter may be. What if devotion startles so because our way of conceiving of *how we know* is only a portion of the path? What if *knowledge* today is partially *faulty*, starving us from the full abundance of awareness possible with human bodies held well in a community able to steward light and dark with compassion?

"Knowledge is never an indifferent, atemporal, aspatial, translucent matrix," Olthuis begins. "There is no such thing as 'Universal Reason—a fixed transtemporal structure that in no way depends on the nature of our bodily experience nor on the social contexts, historical events, or cultural practices in which it is manifested.' Knowledges cannot be and never were neutral, dispassionate, disinterested." Learning to know *other-wise* means exploring another way of knowing, "a way of knowing 'the other' . . . , a knowing of the heart with the eye of love."[1] As he introduces the volume of

---

1. Olthuis, "Introduction: Love/Knowledge," 1. Olthuis quotes Mark Johnson, *Moral Imagination*, 108.

essays, he describes this *way* with more concrete descriptions. It is of the body, meeting, mutuality, intimacy-with not power-over; love; opening, not closure; connection, not fusion; drawing nigh, not distancing; celebrating-with, and suffering-with, the other. Ultimately, "Knowing-otherwise is a spiritual process of mutual transformation in which we release/are released into the Mystery of Love out of which everything arises. Knowing otherwise is to take the risk of loving the other, the risk of meeting in mutuality."[2] Devotion feels like a risk, in this sense, because it is a fullness of knowing beyond our familiar, our comfort zones. It makes a claim on us.

"Knowing of the heart with the eye of love." *Seeing with the heart.* Contemplatives describe this way of seeing, knowing, that today would be judged subjective, counterintuitive, even dangerous: a heart path, emerging from a deepened bodyspace—womb-space for women, root-chakra or lower core for men. I have rarely, if ever, been in an academic or ecclesial setting where this way of *knowing* is taught, how to think from a bodyspace like this. The popular assumption is that thinking is a head thing, an abstracted, even ethereal or spiritual faculty of the human person. As a Presbyterian, I assure you that most in my community have little sense that their bodies offer anything worthwhile. The spirit-flesh dualism given huge voice in the writings of Paul insures a cognitive disdain of the body, of its fidelity to bridging life and death, spirit and earth. In contrast, Tilden Edwards invites a deepened seeing through the heart, encouraging his readers/listeners to "drop their minds into their hearts," a "process of letting the mind sink into the intuitive spiritual heart's desire for true life in God, including a desire for an immediate awareness of Reality shining in the divine Presence."[3] Cynthia Bourgeault names this *seeing with the heart* a new-ancient way for today's disembodied souls to practice, to even begin to see and know the giftedness, the potential within awakening to a journey of the heart in our world.

She observes this journey is *state-dependent*, by which she means related to the entire human-bodied condition for perception and reception. The invitation on offer here, for all of us, is to a "lucid and objective way of seeing that is ultimately visionary." Her sense of the difficulties in awakening is not that our vision has grown too small but "that we are using too little of ourselves to see."[4] She invites us into an intuitive *felt-sense* way of

2. Ibid., 8.
3. Edwards, *Embracing the Call*, loc. 180.
4. Bourgeault, *Wisdom Way of Knowing*, 9.

being in our rapidly paced lives—which feels risky or foreign to our mind-habits today. "To read the clues, it is first necessary to bring the heart and mind and body into balance, to awaken. Then the One can be known—not in a flash of mystical vision but in the clarity of unitive seeing."[5] The practices within which we structure our day will foretell how, what, and even who we see.

Bourgeault notes the Wisdom School practices she and her students engaged regularly—mindful work, sacred chanting, meditation, prayer, etc.—are not just paths of intention (though they are that) for rhythm and balance. These practices or activities are actually "gateways of perception," *floodgates* of perception. So she urges us to lower our minds into our hearts, become truly present to the work of the day—whatever it might be—and find our minds looking outward through our hearts into Presence, right there, right then. As I practice this in my own life, I do find: Presence is always right there, right then. Brother Lawrence was right—Presence needs to be practiced within the ordinary tasks of our day, every day.

So what does this mean in the context of a companionable way? How does one actually enter into the river of devotion, to see first and foremost with the heart? As introductory and obvious as it may sound, you simply begin *in the world*, with *sacred intention* and *humility*, with a *desire* to know, *within the welcomes offered you*. For years Bourgeault led this way in Wisdom schools, which were gently paced residential offerings in which participants engaged mindfully in this fashion. The slow-paced work of community grounded itself in the world in sacred intention, deep listening, contemplative rhythm, mindful work. This companionable way interprets and innovates a little with this idea, inviting short-term immersion in the practices of other wisdom traditions, to offer one's body in humility to the wisdom of another, to see first with the heart, not the mind.

The mindful immersion into practice is a risky pedagogy, in one sense, particularly for practitioners in Christian traditions unaware of imperialist and colonialist histories of cultural appropriation. Hence "short-term" and "learning/teaching environments" alone, ideally companioned with welcoming spirit-friends giving their interpretations and experience along the way. A short-term but genuine surrender of one's own body sense to the wisdom of others can *honor* the wisdom of others, after all, not appropriate it or its culture for one's own. When entered into carefully, with sacred intention and critical sensitivity that then relinquishes the practice/

---

5. Ibid., 10.

observance, such mindful practice allows a seeing with the heart, not solely the intellect.

To give a little structure or framework, I invite a glimpse into the practices shaped by the conceptual categories of space, time, food, body, and speech. These are rather arbitrary, though conceptually grounding and without overt reference to a religious tradition. Culturally, the approach is Western European, of course, with the preference for cognitive abstraction, but the intention is to remove as many scales from the eyes as possible when reflecting upon specific religious practices.

SPACE

The first practice is simply *to bring your body* into the *space* of another community, *when invited*. This can be as simple as stopping into a halal market or an ethnic grocery store of some kind close to your home. These are public places where, usually, anyone is welcome to browse the shelves and make purchases. Other possibilities include visiting a Shabbat eve service in a local synagogue, or Friday afternoon prayers at a local mosque or Muslim center. If you are Jewish or Muslim, it could be entering a Roman Catholic parish for Mass or a Bahá'í worship center. As basic as it sounds, the first step in opening to a companionable way is simply bringing your body into new spaces you identify as "other," as long as they are ones that welcome you to do so.

It's remarkable to me how infrequently many of us—even in the United State of America—venture into spaces that are not religiously, even culturally identifiable as "our own." Many of us do not quite know how to begin, enculturated into our own communities' social norms. Others of us are so exhausted with being in spaces that identify us as "other" that we retreat into "safe" identity spaces. The end result is identifiably homogenous "identity groups" raging or advocating, one against the other. So there *is* an artistry to entrance into multi-identity spaces where all voices can be heard. A welcome or invitation needs to be discerned first, in some fashion. A halal market is a public space requiring less overt discernment, but entering into a community's religious space requires learning first *how to be a perfect stranger*, as one excellent resource names it. How may we learn just enough to enter into the new spaces with humility, respect of others' customs, demonstrated by attempts to know, to respect them *as we enter*? Regardless, each of us brings the "eyes and ears" of our own experience, our own sense of space and its significance in our community. Developing eyes able to see anew, ears able to hear anew, requires new spaces and communities to show us how.

For instance, most Christians I know bring their own implicit assumptions to how they see synagogues or temples within Jewish heritage. "Synagogues look like Christian churches, except they're Jewish," in other words. The center of many Christian traditions is the communal gathering place, the sanctuary, after all. This is where the baptisms happen, and where the sacrament of communion is offered. The strong communal center of Christianity means that the communal gathering place is pivotal, primary in a life of faith. Synagogues feel like this to Christians, many times.

Except the center of Jewish observance is the family table, in the home. Shabbat eve and Shabbat dinners happen here. Passover happens here. The bulk of Jewish observance is overseen and protected by the one at home, traditionally a woman. Yom Kippur, the Day of Atonement, centers in the synagogue, and each holiday offers prayer services in which the community gathers, but the center of gravity in Jewish observance is most often the home, the family table. The rabbis constructed it this way to protect the traditions after the destruction of the temple way back when. Trying to get Christian eyes to see the reverse centrality takes tremendous effort, beginning with the body and seeing with the heart.

So much more happens when you bring your body into a space new to you, after all. I often encourage the conversation necessary to see if a picture or selfie is appropriate or welcome. This is not so much for the picture as it is for the conversation. Some communities welcome the curiosity and sacred openness of others in their space, inviting pictures to be taken. Others require no pictures, to honor the sacred quality, the being-set-apart of their spaces. Either way, when one is willing to enter into a space and, with humility and respect, ask about another's space, doors can open that were previously unexpected. Of course, in our world steeped in fear and distrust, doors may close too. One has to be prepared to encounter others' fears and freedoms, as well as the vulnerability of bringing one's body into the space of another, when invited. *Being there*, however, allows you to see with your heart, not simply your intellect and previous understandings.

TIME

Another angle into a companionable way is to observe how different communities structure time—daily, monthly, and yearly. Just to begin, however, requires looking into the multiplicity of calendars alive and well in the world. Did you know that different traditions operate according to different calendars, completely different calendars? I love asking "What year is it?" to a roomful of curious minds, sharing my own relatively recent awareness of just how many there are . . . and why. I still need to ask my rabbi friend whether his daughters celebrate their birthdays on the Jewish calendar day, or the civic calendar day. Or perhaps birthday celebrations are only a civic thing for his family. The options all exist because the Jewish calendar ebbs and flows around the Gregorian one used for civic purposes. Seeing with the heart, however, requires a sensitivity to time and its shaping of others. Know when Ramadan is, for instance, so you don't invite a Muslim friend observing a fast to lunch during that month.

Most traditions structure each *day* with practices, which, when seen with the heart, can shape outsiders from the inside first. The call to prayer arises fives times a day in Muslim countries, for instance, with attention to precise times and dates. Immersing in *salat* prayer practices—at each timed call to prayer, in this instance—demonstrates the felt sense of this commitment in the variety of cultures and settings unfamiliar with such a daily rhythm. When those curious enough to try it do so, even if for as little as a week, they get a thorough sense of the centrality of prayer for devout Muslims. And they learn how difficult it may be to sustain this commitment in environments largely hostile to Muslim experience and peaceable values (alongside the extremist expressions we see all over the news). In more Western, pluralist environments, these times may implicitly structure a day for a colleague while most of his/her colleagues have little awareness of it. How may we honor the observance of our companions, supporting and co-creating a schedule in which such things are valued—the person over the ideology, the practice over the bottom line? Awareness seems the first step, even to begin to find connection amidst rampant division and disconnection.

A reigning hypothesis for me in the years to come: learning how different communities celebrate life through their holidays may be the best way forward to living into interdependence one and all. You can learn a lot about a community based upon what they celebrate and how. Wouldn't that be a delightful way to begin an interfaith conversation, instead of comparing and contrasting beliefs and cosmologies? Every tradition has their wild party days, with wonderful invitations and amusements too.

BODY

The dimension of the body can challenge our *seeing with the heart* the most. Custom can overwhelm the logical mind in how bodies have traditionally been covered, cared for, arranged in communal spaces. The movement of bodies in prayer communicates unexpected learnings. The invitation I offer those (non-Muslims) seeking deeper connection to their own life of prayer is to pray *salat* for seven days straight. Not only is it organized by a communal schedule, but it involves distinct practices of cleansing and movement—prostration, bowing, standing, speaking. I provide basic instructions but also allow each to find his/her way into the experience of body-prayer. Another invitation is simply to wear head coverings for a period of days, whether male or female. One Buddhist student in a local divinity school, for example, chose to wear a *hijab* for the six weeks of the Christian Lent. She blogged about it, learning "from the inside" what this body-practice brings forth in a secularized overculture. And what she learned was unexpected, counterintuitive even, for a Western woman. So, exploring different body-practices of other wisdom traditions, for just a short time, allows you to bring your mind (and its assumptions and understandings) into your heart to see anew what you might learn.

"Muslims pray so much more than I do!" is a common refrain of Christian students who have engaged the *salat* prayer practice for seven days. Another refrain: "I never realized how disembodied my own prayer life is." The exploration of the *hijab* in a largely secular American environment challenged the popular conception of this practice as only the oppression of women. It certainly can be, perhaps is, but when seen with the heart, from the inside first? It can also be a stand of strength against Western consumerism that objectifies women's bodies. Hijabi women stand behind a veil of their choosing, saying *no* to the buy-and-sell fashions of a consumer-driven marketplace constructed around the male gaze, the objectification of women's bodies. I found sacred shelter myself in prayer once, praying underneath a headscarf during Friday afternoon prayers at a local Muslim center. Completely unexpected, deeply sacred, I *got* some of the power of the privacy enabled within a veil. A veil that *I chose*, which was significant, but there was a sacred wisdom I learned within it.

A Companionable Way

FOOD

The origin of most of this framework for *seeing with the heart* was an intuitive practice project of Jewish immersion: maintaining a kosher home—as best I could—for four weeks during my tradition's Lenten season. The final two weeks were spent non-kosher, reading Pauline scripture, to see if it "read" differently afterward. It did. You can read about it more thoroughly in the essay it produced, but bringing my body into the observance of another wisdom tradition—surrendering to its wisdom without giving priority to my own tradition's defenses—transformed my encounters with every Jewish person I have met since.

I was experimenting with the notion of space and the contradictions I was experiencing between Christian and Jewish prioritization of space. I was awakening (slowly) to the centrality of the family table within Jewish observance, though synagogue services were complementary for most, of course. So often, Christian presumption imposes itself into Jewish space and observance, so I found myself wondering: What would it feel like to have Jewish wisdom at the center of my own home, the presence of another faith tradition guiding my own life for a spell?

It was incredibly disorienting, destabilizing, not a little overwhelming. Every meal, each utensil in the kitchen, needed mindful attention. My family relationships stretched and strained a little, as I changed my eating and meal practices. I began to internalize pieces of rabbinic wisdom and more contemporary custom, startled when they arose as judgment or distinction from other levels of observance. It was simply fascinating, and deeply compelling. I became a convert, of sorts, to *kashrut* wisdom, though I was also relieved when my four weeks were over. All that I read to understand, all the conversations I had to learn about kosher—none of it compared to bringing my mind into my heart and my heart into the observance within my body. *Seeing with the heart* allowed me entrance into communal wisdom I had not *felt* so deeply before. Even now, I can grow a little wistful for the sense of order and sacred interconnection I knew when observing *kashrut*, though I am also relieved it is not a practice within my own tradition.

Within this framework, then, I invite those interested to explore the food practices observed in other traditions. Sometimes it means becoming vegetarian and learning the reasons why. Buddhist wisdom, for instance. Other times, it can mean fasting on certain days and feasting on others. In any case, becoming familiar with the levels of observance in other traditions can ease civic and communal gatherings. Providing a welcome for *everyone* at a common meal can mean at least insuring there is no bacon in the green beans. Or welcoming a rabbi to oversee the production in the kitchen so food acquisition and preparation meet hospitable and healthy practice.

SPEECH

The final area of practice or listening is traditionally the one we spend *all* our time in when learning to encounter an "other" in our midst. All these words are a practice of speech, for instance. Most communities today have "dialogues" and "trialogues" to engage conversations about traditions across difference. When prefaced with weeks of other explorations—space, time, body, food—the flatness of speech becomes apparent for truly *seeing with the heart*, however. As Bourgeault said above, "How you are working or feeling will shape how and what you see." If we jump into speech before we've brought our bodies into the spaces, times, customs, and food practices of others, we have not honored them with the time, the humility, the surrender to their own wisdom. We will always be speaking within our own categories. Still, an express willingness to be changed by the wisdom of another can lead to open hearts and different speech, deeper listening together. Remember, these practices or activities are "gateways of perception," even floodgates of perception. Each time I extend the invitations into deeper body practices before moving into the dance and parry of speech, students awaken to the superficial ways they had been "seeing" the world. They often emerge humbled and curious, with a gentler passion for their own tradition's practices and wisdom.

CONCLUSION

Choosing to dive deeply into this stream in a world dead set against its pace, rhythms, and invitations is costly. Traveling with others at a metaphorical thirty thousand miles an hour in speech allows you to feel part of a crowd, even if it's a hungry, tired, and weary crowd. Dropping to an inch off the ground, moving at the pace of guidance,[6] means you drop out of sight, out of the limited awareness of your previous traveling companions. First it feels incredibly lonely, fearful, and who wants to choose to be *there*? In

---

6. Baldwin, *Seven Whispers*, 23–38.

Bourgeault's words, "Such seeing is costly ... It requires the whole of one's being and is ultimately attained only through the yielding of one's whole being." The first sensations are often a yielding into that loneliness, a quiet one cannot control or fathom. Julia Cameron speaks of this moment in creative renewal too. "Leap, and the net will appear."[7] You don't see the net first, then decide. You don't see the abundance or devotion and then choose to enter in. You sense nothingness first. Loneliness that, in time, and only in its own time, becomes solitude. Which paradoxically leads you right into an overwhelming intimacy with oneself, the world, and those who then are simply, seemingly irresistibly, drawn to you, or better, the river of devotion that can come through you. In Bourgeault's full words, then: "Such seeing ... requires the whole of one's being and is ultimately attained only through the yielding of one's whole being into the intimacy of knowing and being known. ... It doesn't happen apart from complete vulnerability and self-giving. But the divine Lover is absolutely real, and for those willing to bear the wounds of intimacy, the knowledge of that underlying coherence—'in which all things hold together'—is both possible and inevitable."[8] The "wounds of intimacy" names the sensation just so, in my experience.

And then you find yourself in what Olthuis calls "sojourning together in the wild spaces of love,"[9] a journey of mutuality that re-envisions *love* out of its modern captivities in power or knowledge. This vision of love re-envisions the spaces and containers within which new life may grow. Such a journey of devotion arises from seeing with the heart, which *happens* to those who are willing. The doorway into its invitations is less a conscious pursuit of spiritual practices and techniques and much more an easing of the mind into a space you fear to go—an outer space that feels other but is yet inviting you, and an inner space, deep within yourself, which then pushes you back into the world to offer what you didn't think you could do in the first place. Welcome to the world of *choiceless choice*, a relinquishing of what you thought you were doing in order to become a receptacle and vehicle for what you could not have imagined.

---

7. Cameron, *Artist's Way*, 42.
8. Bourgeault, *Wisdom Way of Knowing*, 10.
9. Olthuis, "Crossing the Threshold," 245.

Rebirthing

Nearly ten years into this companionable way, a sacred circle brought me whole in a way previously inconceivable to me as a theology professor. I offer it here because fundamental to this path of devotion in conscious love is a return to the body, neglected and dissociated in most educational settings. This journey to the body's wisdom unexpectedly disorients and reorients, both at the same time, and few institutions of education I know today are prepared to lead the way to this kind of knowing, this depth of awakening. Yet only at this vulnerable human door will devotion be born, borne. The circle that spontaneously led me to this awakening was familiar to me, but I had never been so close to its fierce wisdom and healing energies.

The circle began to gather, having enjoyed over an hour of "being-time": eating, resting, talking, walking, returning women to their bodies, slowing down to listen, to hold, to enter into sacred space. We spoke ourselves into the circle, immersed more deeply into sensate awareness by means of a guided meditation. Then ten minutes of pair-sharing followed, each woman holding the words and "emotional placedness" of the other for five minutes. The large circle came to itself again, and the invitation arrived for each of us to speak and be seen, have our words of intention held. One woman chose a talking piece from the center table, offered herself and her words for us to hold, to celebrate. Another followed her. A song began and came to its conclusion.

Finally, I felt the nudge to take my turn. I chose the originating circle-stone for this community, held it in my hands while I knelt in the circle to offer up what words would come. "It seems odd," I began, "to name some of this into a circle with mothers and midwives, but I now know why I have never wanted to have children." I could feel heat rising, arriving in my cheeks, my neck. "I have sat these last few weeks with an infant picture of mine—an infant selfie, we might say—to try to receive and learn from my body what I need to receive, to know. Deep pain is there, I have learned—fear, sadness, isolation, rage. No wonder I avoid holding infants, let alone the body labor to bring one into the world from within me." A quiet presence gave me pause. "I am learning to re-mother myself, to allow my body awareness of its pain and to release it. My intention for this month, therefore, is to deepen my capacity and skills to companion my preverbal self, who needs so desperately to be held." A couple of tears dropped onto my chest, but I smiled, returning the circle-stone to the center as signal I was nearly finished speaking. I offered thanksgiving to the circle, without whom I would not be doing this work, I suspected, and returned to my place in the outer rim. Someone began to sing a chantlike prayer-song we often sing in this circle of women: *I will believe the truth about myself, no matter how beautiful it is.* I smiled, tearing up a little more.

What I was *not* prepared for, however, was my friend, a midwife in training, looking into my face with deep delight, asking, "Do you want to be *born*?" She might have said *reborn*, but neither of us can recall now. My brow furrowed and I looked at her, waiting for more detail. Within moments, all the midwives of the circle surrounded me with smiles and overwhelming, abundant joy on their faces. "Lisa!" they said, each in turn, in a voice I recognized as one reserved for infants. "We are so glad you are here. Welcome, welcome, welcome! What a beautiful little girl and look at those fingers!" One touched my hands, spending time with each finger. Another touched my toes, wriggling them for me, gently holding them in the palms of her hands. Another touched my face, a look of wonder and welcome pouring forth from her into me. The singing held us all as they laughed and smiled and touched and *welcomed me.* The tears and laughter erupting out of me came without thought or word.

It was the most hilariously foolish and fiercely sacred thing I can remember happening to me, to all of me. More than my Christian baptism, which I remember. More than my ordination into the Presbyterian clergy, which I remember. My little infant-girl self was welcomed into the world, as a girl, in the most fiercely feminine fashion. I could never have conceived of a welcome like this one. *She's back,* I heard inside my soul, with a smile.

I sat for a long time in that space, after the circle completed its listening and various pairs and trios huddled to make plans for the upcoming week or clear dirty dishes from the space. Not every circle that gathers is that hilariously ebullient or fiercely intimate, you should know. The containers are co-created by those willing to take on the particular energies and needs of those who show up. But something in the archetypal energies of the circle, co-created by this gathering of women, wove it all together in an innovative, spontaneous ritual of healing, a (re)birth of a credentialed theology professor returning—being returned—to her body. Rebirthing.

A Companionable Way

How might your life have been different if,
    in the beginning,
        there were a place for you as a little one of deep feeling

where desire was not dark, dangerous, destructive
    but awakening, inviting, and light
        connecting all of you to yourself, your family, others
            without shame, without fear . . .

where being seen and mirrored in love flowed without thought,
    being held in darkness and light was the most natural way of becoming

where *everything* that arose could be welcomed deeply in your own body,
    attuned to the bodies around you
        where you received your innate giftedness, goodness, and purpose
            as your birthright?

            How might your life have been different?
            How might our world be different?

Awakening

"It was a pleasure to burn," begins Ray Bradbury's *Fahrenheit 451*, an unexpected glimpse into a felt sense of *awakening*. Though it's a classic, I had never read it until I was nearly forty, when I read it twice in one week. It touched something deep within me, describing something I recognized but had been a little afraid of saying aloud or naming to those I love. Not that I felt the government was going to come pick me up for sitting in meditation practice with Tibetan Buddhists, or for sitting in the observance and "benching" prayer of Jews, but I knew my Christian community would sure raise eyebrows at what I was doing in either place, as a Christian. So with Montag, goaded into awakening by Clarisse, I could begin to put another's words to both the giddy delight and deep belly fear that were shaping my journey.

I knew I was where my heart was leading me, as a person of faith, where I was being Led, but each experience of new and unintended encounter felt risky, potentially difficult. The encounter in a Jewish shtiebel offered me an intense deepening of connection and compassion with my new Jewish friends, for instance, *and* that encounter was painful, destabilizing, enraging. *Awakening*, truly *entering in* to an encounter, in other words, is something that sounds virtuous and noble—something we want or ought to do—but the actual felt sense of it can be disruption, fear, and aversion—a groundlessness that most of us as human beings resist and avoid. It therefore has to arrive *indirectly*, outside our conscious choice, as in my case with a science fiction classic by Ray Bradbury.

Awakening arrives indirectly with Montag, the book-burning "fireman" in Bradbury's classic. He burns books for a living, because they contradict one another, they confuse ordinary people with too much knowledge. He meets a young woman, Clarisse, who innocently asks him the question of happiness, meaning. What he says is not as important as the felt sense of her question, landing in his body: "He felt his body divide itself into a hotness and coldness, a softness and hardness, a trembling and a not trembling, the two halves grinding one upon the other."[1] His awakening has begun, and it's not easy or pleasant.

He finds himself sneaking books to read, unable to quench this hunger growing deep inside. Eventually, of course, fleeing the authorities who have identified his "treason," he finds himself on the outskirts of town. He sees something strange, unexpected—familiar yet also foreign. "Half an hour later . . . fully aware of his entire body . . . he saw the fire ahead. That small motion, the white and red color, a strange fire because it meant a different thing to him. It was not burning, it was *warming*." He stands, watching and sensing for a long time. "How long he stood he did not know, but there was a foolish and yet delicious sense of knowing himself. . . . It was not only the fire that was different. It was the silence. Montag moved toward this special silence that was concerned with all the world."[2] In precise fictional fashion, Montag awakens to a new way of seeing, a new pursuit of knowledge through a deeply sensate and difficult journey. Outside his current communal center, he discovers a strange fire held within a ragged community of fellow travelers, a silence concerned with all the world.

Reading these words today, I can see why I read the book through twice in one week. The awakening to living wisdom outside of, yet intimately related to, my own tradition seemed "a strange fire." The "work of silence" had found me too, first with the Quakers (Society of Friends), but then with Buddhists, then within the work of Maggie Ross.[3] There seemed to be a force of Life taking precedence in my life over my image and expectation of what my work would be. A portion of it felt like "awakening in public," as my teaching became contemplative, then an interweaving circle-way of learning, not unlike sitting around a strange fire in the center. It was a remarkable and reorienting energy of felt Invitation in which preparing for my seminary coursework in the staid old ways and administering details of a formation program were important but not the point or the purpose, the direction or the demand. So I did what I always used to do in these matters. I went to the library to learn what others have learned before me.

I received comfort and sustenance with Robert Ullman and Judyth Reichenberg-Ullman's writing on awakening. They offer an initial

---

1. Bradbury, *Fahrenheit 451*, 53.
2. Ibid., 171–72.
3. Ross, *Silence*, 1:38–65.

description of the human phenomenon of awakening available to us in concrete lives as various as the Buddha, Catherine of Siena, John of the Cross, Kabir, the Baal Shem Tov, and contemporary American-global sages.[4] In this compilation of historical writings and stories, they define *awakening* simply as the provision of knowledge or spiritual insight, illumination, even enlightenment.[5] "Those who describe enlightenment experiences recount a shift out of their ordinary frames of reference," they write. "Their worldviews become markedly different. . . . This alteration leaves these enlightened beings in a state of freedom. They are still themselves, and yet they are not. . . . They are absolutely free, and extraordinarily awakened."[6] Several features emerge in this phenomenological view of awakening.

The shift in awareness from previous frames of reference into one of *interconnectedness* marks one aspect of awakening. "This shift may be described as the dissolution of the self, a merging of the wave in the ocean, union with the infinite, abdication of the personal sense of doership, or loss of a separate identity."[7] This requires *ego transcendence* or a sense of releasing identification in terms of self, ego, or personality. A second characteristic of awakening in these stories is *timelessness and spaciousness*. Awakening realizes a "moment-to-moment" existence in which the present moment is all there is and concepts of time and space are fluid. A relaxation or surrender manifests a third characteristic, *acceptance*. "Struggle ends and gives way to acceptance of a reality free of bondage from and attachment to personal desires, thoughts, and feelings."[8] Living into a space *beyond pleasure and pain* typifies many stories of awakening. Those who have experienced it describe ecstasy, rapture, and love that transcends suffering, though some also describe a fear, confusion, disorientation, pain, even madness that may last over a period of time. In the authors' typology here, pleasure and "suffering exist but the personal identification . . . does not."[9] The final two characteristics they identify in their compilation of stories are *clarity* and the *shattering of preconceived notions*. "The enlightened mind is spontaneous, immediate and flexible. . . . Rigidity, expectations, preconceived ideas

---

4. Ullman and Reichenberg-Ullman, *Mystics, Masters, Saints, and Sages*, xv–xx.
5. Ibid., xv–xviii.
6. Ibid., xv.
7. Ibid., xvii.
8. Ibid.
9. Ibid., xviii.

and personae give way to a vaster reality and even to a profound realization of emptiness, vastness, or nothingness."[10]

These features are intended not as a systematic construction of awakening in its essence, of course. The Ullmans remind their readers and I reiterate it: "No two experiences [of enlightenment] are ever the same." Their compilation, and the bulk of the work in these pages, aims to simply suggest a path of awakening with recognizable aspects in human experience. It comes with a heady title—*Mystics, Masters, Saints, and Sages*—but the journey they describe need not be all that magnanimous or perceivedly glorious. It's not only mystics, masters, saints, and sages who *awaken*, in other words. The felt sense of it bears little resemblance to our perception of it from a book, which is admirable, virtuous, therefore desirable. The *experience* of awakening as I have received and witnessed it is disruptive, fearful, groundless. One of aversion, surrender, loss of control over life. Who *chooses* that?

The description of awakening follows what others have called a "logic of discovery" or even a "transformational logic," to use the phrase of my own teacher, James E. Loder. I found in their "signs of awakening" an understanding potentially helpful for inviting myself and others into a deepening journey of faith. Crafting a "curriculum" of peer-group learning with a confessional Christian base, I yet found myself propelled into multiple deepening spiritual intimacies with diverse traditional friends (or those with no named tradition at all). Overwhelming interconnectedness. Unexpected transcendence (or transfiguration) of who I knew myself to be. Timelessness and spaciousness to receive, to offer and give of myself, my time, my heart. Acceptance of myself but also the irreconcilable differences I encountered, trusting way would open for deepening the holy invitations between companions—*and it always has*. Sensate awareness beyond pleasure and pain, an interwoven journey of yearning and devotion, with all the complexities that accompany them. Struggle or wrestling, resistance to this devotion deepening in sensate awareness can create suffering, of course, a sense of restlessness and even pain, but it is one of interconnection and grief at suffering, not isolation or fear. Clarity and the shattering of preconceived notions. Amen to that. Not only am I doing work I had never conceived of or imagined, but there is a quiet clarity that the work will be done in me however it needs to be. God is not remotely who I thought S/he was and yet is revealed again and again in ways incontrovertibly recognizable.

10. Ibid., xvii–xviii.

Awakening

One companion whose journey joined my own for many of these years describes one of his awakenings in a similar way, with familiar language. An eighth-generation rabbi of Conservative Jewish hue, Irwin Kula was startled on the morning of September 11th to a calling for us to "teach religion differently than we've been taught." He saw the incendiary destruction of the Twin Towers' falling, losing several dear friends as they fell, and knew there was something about how religion is traditioned that contributed to the overwhelming violence. His journey into what my own tradition might call "a dark night of the soul" led him to traditionally rooted yet innovative writing and teaching with collaborations instigated by his book *Yearnings: Embracing the Sacred Messiness of Life*. I met him when this book landed in my seminary mailbox; to this day neither of us knows how I got on the list. Listening for what he calls "humble absolutes," he described a moment of awakening that happened in an unusual context for a rabbi—in the pews of a church. "For traditional Jews," he begins,

> entering churches is forbidden. I was forty-two years old when I went into one for the first time. I'd passed by the same beautiful old church on my way to work for many years; then early one morning some small voice within me urged me to go in. As I sat in the wooden pew I was engulfed by unfamiliar sights and smells: incense, candles burning, light streaming in through stained glass windows. And then I looked up at the crucifix, a cross with a corpus, the figure of Jesus bleeding from the heart. As I meditated on this central symbol of Christianity for the first time, I was horrified, struck by thoughts about centuries of Christian persecution of Jews. I wanted to run away. My palms were sweating, and I had to hold on to the side of the pew in order to make myself stay. I kept looking and looking, thinking there just had to be something more here than my own tradition's perspective.
>
> It could have been fifteen minutes or forty-five minutes, but I suddenly found myself thinking, "What if my heart was that open? What if I could feel everyone's pain, so much so that my heart exploded?" I understood in a flash the meaning of sacred heart. And I heard the words from a prayer I'd said every day since I was a boy, in a whole new way: "*Karov YHWH L'nishberai Lev*," God is Close to the Brokenhearted. I didn't convert that day, but my God got an awful lot bigger. And so did I.[11]

---

11. Kula and Loewenthal, *Yearnings*, 14.

Moment after moment, just like this, erupted for us in the years of collaboration Irwin and I shared—guest lecturing, team-teaching a seminary course, leading events in a local congregational context. This "small voice" of invitation. The intense aversion, even disgust, that can arise when what is sacred to one tradition faces or enters into the heart of someone from another tradition. Centuries of violence and fear—otherizing and slaughter—arise in the psychological energies we experienced, and we faced impulses of "fight or flight." When we could stay with the energy, the fear—when it was safe to do so—then again and again, we found insight and transfiguration to erupt into awareness, understanding, but more importantly, *heart-connection*. Seeing with the heart.

In sum, *awakening* rarely happens when we expect it, nor can we craft or create it. Wisdom traditions may describe it in terms we find noble, virtuous, clearly desirable, but its realities are quite different in the felt sense. Groundlessness, disruption, senselessness amidst previous frames of reference—each of these is a harbinger of actual awakening. Much as David Schnarch describes intimacy—not for the faint of heart—so awakening challenges everything we hold dear for the sake of a deeper love, a broader vision, a further future.

While it's not for the faint of heart, each of us has more heart for it than we know, particularly as we open ourselves to friendships from unexpected directions. When held within the strong container of companionship, strongly held within circle energies, awakening allows us to enter into encounters we do not conceive. If we truly enter in, we find and are found in a well of devotion, a way of the heart, promising more abundance, vibrancy, and significance than any of us within older traditional structures can easily imagine.

Deepening—Into the Dark of Initiation

I drove nearly a thousand miles one July weekend to place a pomegranate at the gravestone of a woman I'd never met. She had died in 1941, nearly thirty years before my birth. Elizabeth M. Musser Hess she is to me in history. Wife of Abram Z., my great-grandfather, mother of Benjamin M., my paternal grandfather. She was just "Elizabeth M." to me then—a feminine enigma whose life, stories, and voice had been hidden from me by time and circumstance. Everyone I encountered along the way supposed I was going for my father's cousin Wilmer's memorial service. I played along. What else could I have said? "I'm here to leave a pomegranate at the gravestone of a woman who died in 1941"? Standing there at her graveside, I still wasn't sure why I had come, though I did bring the pomegranate.

Wilmer had sought me out in the five years before his passing, to plant his passion for the Musser-Hess history. I did not come to know him well, but I was glad for his letters, the snippets of story and the photographs he would send. Our correspondence waxed and waned as life moved us both onward. Which is why the inner nudge to consider attending his memorial service, several hundred miles away, perplexed me. The idea of it simply would not let me go. I contacted his daughter, to give "my regrets that I could not come," figuring that would take care of it. The idea of going took deeper root. I went to my stack of archetypal images, an intuitive practice of mine to learn more about felt senses that arise in my body. The image that arose made me gasp. A woman, both young and old, was holding a pomegranate at the center of her white-lined robe. Sacred heart, I saw first. A blood-red pomegranate at the center of the cross her white robes fashioned. The instant I saw the image, I knew I was going, though I had no idea why. I remembered Sue Monk Kidd's book *Traveling with Pomegranates*, a travel diary written in collaboration with her daughter. I picked up a copy, as companion and symbol of this intuitive, counterintuitive journey unfolding. Where could I find a pomegranate?

The next day, five hundred miles away, I found myself a short distance from the memorial service, at the same hotel as my parents, who had come for obvious reason. Dad knew Wilmer well, from early life into later years. The morning of the service, we tailgated together, driving in tandem to the church. We arrived early enough to visit the cemetery where our ancestors were buried. Dad took my picture by the gravestone, then motioned us into the church. "The service is beginning soon," he said.

We sat in the back row, and I made sure I had a seat on the aisle. Something was drawing me outside and I knew I wouldn't be staying in the service itself. "Wilmer would understand," I whispered to Dad, hoping my quiet exit could be private, solitary. Leaving the sanctuary quietly, I drew near to the gravestones in the churchyard. An overwhelming aroma of chocolate wafted into my awareness, bringing a smile and the felt sense of a circle-sister. She had once written a stunning poem about chocolate, laced with sacramental imagery. Amidst the many, I found the gravestone I had been seeking. I learned at least one reason I had come.

To weep. Searing, deep-belly sobs, forceful and unbidden, rose out of me. I removed my sandals, took off my jacket, raised my face to the drops of rain that were misting the air. I placed the pomegranate on the lower edge of the gravestone, close to the Elizabeth M. I had come to meet. Whatever else I had expected on this journey, this was not it. Rage, grief, anger poured out of my eyes, nose, mouth. Clearly my own, but also somehow *not* my own.

"She doesn't even have her own fucking gravestone," I heard myself say. In my mind's image, I had had two tombstones—his and hers. But there was only one. A not uncommon practice, particularly for a community of simplicity and sparse resources. But the weight of "Hess" engraved into it seemed to push her down further and further into the granite. I could not reach her. I had rarely heard stories of the women in my family, I realized, though archives and church historical works often cited the words of the men. "*His wife*," the stone said next. It seemed that only the stone was speaking. Cold. Ritualistic. Encased in role and rock. And I wondered at the M. What does the M. stand for? The Pennsylvania Deutsch practice was for children to receive, as their middle name, the maiden name of the mother. A week later, when the archival information arrived at my request, I learned Elizabeth was the daughter of Michael Brenner Musser and Catherine Newcomer Musser. I had never heard of Catherine before. Elizabeth should then be Elizabeth N. Musser, noting her mother's maiden name Newcomer. In this history, Newcomer bowed to Musser, precluding the motherline once again. Engraved in stone, she became Elizabeth M.

A week and two days later, I set apart the Sabbath Sunday as a day of mourning, of receiving the rage I felt at knowing so very little of the motherline in which I stand. I placed nothing but a blank tile picture on my Facebook page, an act others had done in protest of something else but which for me was a public act of mourning. Facelessness. Disregard of the forgotten. Standing in a sacred but empty yurt, a gathering place of circles of women, I spoke the names of my motherline aloud: Martha Engle, Elizabeth Brenner, Catherine Newcomer, Elizabeth N. Musser, Ruth Berger, Carol Virginia. I will not forget you, I said to myself silently.

I welcome each of them into my awareness, my listening. Together, we sit eating a little box of dark-chocolate-covered pomegranate seeds, smiling to have been lost but now found. All it ever takes is a little tenacity, a little courage, and willingness to release the angers of what was in order to welcome the stunning beauty of what is, what can be. Sweet, tart seeds, covered in the most exquisite dark chocolate. Each time I hold a circle of women coming together to come to voice, to deepen their listening, a small container of chocolate-covered pomegranate seeds sits there in the circle. Thank you, Elizabeth Newcomer Musser, and welcome into the circle.

A Companionable Way

"How might your life have been different if there were a place for you,
    a place for you to go,
        to be with your mother,
            with your sisters and the aunts,
                with your grandmothers, and
                    the great- and great-great-grandmothers?
A place of women to go, to be, to return to, as woman?"[1]

And what if that place were the very origin, seed, and blossom of
    the path to devotion, in the flow of conscious love, which

looked nothing like you have been told by those you love,
    asked more willingness than any of you knew you had, and
        required you to give up the certainty cherished by so many?

What if *that* was the very path to becoming the most whole and human being
    you never knew was possible?

        How might your life have been different?
        How might our world be different?

---

1. Duerk, *Circle of Stones*, 19.

A New-Old Sacred

The consciousness holding and bringing a companionable and circling life into the world roots itself and blossoms in diverse ways outside of most traditional institutions today, whether religious, political, or civic. The pathway to this consciousness is therefore intimate and diverse, dependent upon willingness, intention, circumstance, and opportunity. It requires finding a centering place outside of most institutions while retaining enough leverage within them to remain comprehensible to one's peers and colleagues—hence, grounding in exile, befriending outsiders, fidelity in fear of betrayal, and more. This consciousness can even be variously named, though I know its name as the *conscious feminine* or *sacred feminism*, with *sacred* somewhat reconceived away from traditional use. Related to various expressions of today's feminisms, this conscious feminine is also underneath or outside of academic feminism. It is more a willing wordlessness beckoning to something deep within each of us, male or female or in between, inviting each of us to come to speech as may come. This chapter points to the receptive ground and counterbalanced Divine that held my entrance into the path of devotion in conscious love, defining and illustrating as best I can (in words) the new-old sacred that creates and holds space for a companionable circle-way.

FEMININE . . . IN BOTH WOMEN AND MEN

For now, I am standing with the Jungians, using the word *feminine* to mean psychological-spiritual characteristics within both men and women: radical hospitality, wordless presence, open-ended receptivity, tactile affection, fierce gentleness, and a sacred that is deeply embodied and listens without interpretation, judgment, or projection. And of course, patience, kindness, generativity, spacious invitation into deeper and deeper learning of Self and other. Men have these traits. Women have these traits. They are traits for holding spaces, creating relational architecture for people to become aware and responsible for their own journey into deeper human being. These traits expressed allow seeds of masculine energies and directiveness, purpose, linear achievement, and more to have a space in which to germinate, to root, to blossom, to be sent into the world. I have used few of these terms up to this point, especially *feminine*, because the language hits such a deep wound that you will rarely be heard once that rawness is touched. No one wants to be overly associated with it, it seems. I understand, as I disdained all things feminine—which meant weak, inferior, silenced—for decades. That said, I have now gotten curious about the overwhelming energies people have with the word *feminine*. Why does it incite such energy, but for its neglect, fear, aversion?

My unsought, unexpected entrance into devotion—which I now know as the *conscious feminine* rebirthed and dancing alongside a life-giving, conscious masculine—required women birthing consciousness in women, held in circle-way communities. None of it happened in a single moment of birth or rebirth. Neither was it an intellectual feat of insight to be found in any way I had been trained to seek. Unlike I'd been socialized to conceive of it, this was not a journey of discourse and insight for a woman into a new understanding. I have not been proceeding as a woman into what is logically pro-woman, feminist, or woman-centric in defiant opposition to patriarchy or the unconscious masculine. No. More often than not, traditions and even the feminist-womanist-mujeristic contributions—without which so many of us could not have awakened to our deepest Selves as women—are yet received within structural and systemic expectations not unlike "add woman and stir," or "replace man with woman, then bake."

The conscious feminine, or participation in the sacred Feminine, is not like that in my own journey, nor does living within this flow require such articulation. One of the most difficult things for me to name in this journey into devotion is that this invitation and discipline do not necessarily contradict or compete with all that has come before. This F/feminine transfigures, complements, opens a third way to see what before had been oppositional or irreconcilable. She holds an expansive space in which the gifts of masculine and feminine may weave together, grow in refinement with one another. The conscious feminine does not require us to choose for or against, for the Divine Feminine or *not* for Her. Her Love liberates, loves

A New-Old Sacred

without ego, without demand. And She *does* provide for every need, every question, in Her own time. Only in a way of the heart, deeply grounded in the body, however, will She be found, or will this rebalancing journey invited in each of us break ground.

This journey of awakening is open to both men and women because it is a return to the body's wisdom, a gradual unfolding of insights over time and intention, circle spaces and surrender. Anyone with a body and a willingness to be deeply initiated into its abundance and groundedness within and across the gender line can find a peaceable way of becoming uniquely human across irreconcilable difference. That said, it is not *biologically* gendered. The journeys of men and women will be different from one another within this flow, but human wholeness rises only with a recovery of the feminine in both men and women, and each of us in between.

So, in a fashion rather counter to politically correct either-ors, the new-old sacred that has found me on this journey requires a prioritization of the feminine, so to balance the overactive, often unconscious masculine in today's communal settings. No one—men or women—has any reason to lean into conscious femininity until those awakening to its need, gifts, and skills lead in this fashion, risk the consequences for changing the container, stand firm in what they know that contrasts so greatly with the surrounding culture. Participation in this feminine is a deeply embodied, tactile, affectionate, pure, sensual, actively receptive way of being that leads through creating space, not filling it; wordlessness that welcomes voice, doesn't require it; responsiveness, not direction or reaction. Women being with women is how I was initiated into it, without sexual undercurrents (though it is certainly feasible for those currents to arise). Today's socialized masculinity can be initiated in simply being receptive, grounding in the body, learning to listen and respond. But those awakening to the conscious feminine within need to prioritize this Feminine, dare we lose track of its contributions to peaceable encounter.

Deeply intimate, this sensate awareness is reliant upon a person's ability to name and provide—or find provision—for his/her own needs in balance with others. This practice of being in the world, interdependent and receptive, is a grounded, grounding, cyclical and restorative way that Earth knows herself, has known longer than Time written by men. Women take the lead here, though in a fashion often unseen as leadership in the reigning overculture. As a woman learns to name and provide for her own need, so each of us learns to do the same for ourselves. Not "on behalf of" someone else—no one can ever do another's inner work like that—but for oneself, in balance of me and we. Women need to model as they learn, leading in a fashion unexpected but direly needed.

Devotion in conscious love, the path of awakening into the conscious feminine in balance with the conscious masculine, also has a clear religious and/or spiritual character, though it is less like a stream of tradition as conceived today. It is more like an unknowing horizon beckoning wholeness for those with hearts and minds open enough to consider it, steady enough to welcome the holy dark of their own wounds into unexpected healing within deep-listening companionship. Surrender and willingness are necessary to receive the invitation to *not* name, to *not* envision a destination or solution except for immediate availability and practiced listening presence. This is not a traditionally religious pathway, to be sure, in the multiple levels of meaning there. The journey of Christian discipleship that led me into this awakening does not resemble what most Christians in Midwestern America today would call "discipleship." I certainly understand that, though I refuse the projection of infidelity. When I bother with adjectives, I still claim *Christian* for myself. I know who and the One Whose I am, which is sufficient for today. But at a more subtle level, this devotion bears little resemblance to "religion" or "tradition" as they have been conceived, prescribed, and implemented within patriarchal centuries.

The resourcing and support structures have had to be sizeable for me to awaken in this fashion to a soul of the feminine, to choose this new-old awareness of being every day, or even every moment I can retain consciousness of it. Beginning slowly, with seeds planted sporadically along the way: by an elementary school teacher and librarian, both of whom nourished me; a professional woman I met in my senior year of high school; my first job of teaching at a girls' school whose mission was *for girls*; learning with women mentors, then clinical pastoral education supervised by a Sister of Charity and a Quaker, both women. I am learning that it is an everyday calling for someone like me. It is a daily choice, to be consciously enacted again and again in the face of overwhelming, if polite, disavowal of the feminine, by those who love me dearly but who have little experience of what I mean when I say *feminine*.

My struggle is tinged with empathy for my family, of course, because how could they welcome what or who they've seemingly never experienced or known themselves, deeply in body and soul? My beloved grandmother Ruth was really an emperor in so many ways. A cross-dressing Patriarch.

A New-Old Sacred

This is the seed of the struggle for me, I see now. I love all these foibled, flawed human beings with whom I was born. Yet we are all complicit in the abandonment of little girls, of the young feminine in each of us, of the older feminine, of the elder Feminine. Rarely, in any spacious way, has anyone in my family allowed the body—especially a woman's body—to have its own mysterious voice, its own dark wisdom, its own role in sacred connection. Rarely in our midst does the wordless find a place, do the words of women as women come to voice.

The journey for me has been into a way of the heart, a decades-long meander of *return to the body*, my own body, learning to listen for the still small voice of God deep within my own cells, within women's mysteries so long hidden in centuries of inflicted shame. The journey has been a painful one of a woman coming Home to Herself, having been unaware that she was missing at all. It hurts to be pushed outside of any mainstream, any gathering or circle in which you discover you do not belong as you had first supposed. It hurts even more to realize you have been complicit in it yourself, unaware, unconscious, unseen. Even so, this journey of awakening to a way of the heart, to new life in the Feminine, is irrevocably audible and upheld within historic wisdom traditions, if not in the direct fashion so touted in disciplinary work today. The conscious feminine is always indirect, unseen, peripheral and holding. Like the famous "coming to faith" story of Christian apologist C. S. Lewis, for example.

BRIDGE BUILDING—COMING TO FAITH . . .

A famous quote of C. S. Lewis points to both continuity and discontinuity in a coming to faith within a sacred Feminine frame. A longtime atheist and twentieth-century scholar of medieval poetry, he described his "coming to faith" story in a way well suited to an academic ego finding a moment of surrender, as he was to find it again and again within a life of Christian discipleship. "You must picture me alone in that room at Magdalen," he said, "night after night, feeling, whenever my mind lifted even for a second from my work, the steady, unrelenting approach of Him whom I so earnestly desired not to meet. That which I greatly feared had at last come upon me. In the Trinity Term of 1929 I gave in, and admitted that God was God, and knelt and prayed: perhaps, that night, the most dejected and reluctant convert in all England."[1] Rereading these words for the first time in several

---

1. Lewis, *Surprised by Joy*, 266.

years, maybe even decades, I couldn't help smiling at the tenacity of ego and the intimate moment of surrender. If he was going to be a convert to this God, at least he was going to be "the most" in some fashion an intellectual could stomach. Nonetheless, his words do give a glimpse of this intimate relinquishment of self into the reality and care of the Sacred, the terrifying yet holy moment of leaning into Someone or Something larger and more inviting than a human ego is (finally) willing or able to withstand.

This moment, caught in autobiographical time of Lewis's recall, signifies much to many contemporary Christians today—the reality of their (our) God, the legitimacy and validity of their (our) faith, the call of Christ to a certain kind of life or way of being within traditional Christianity. And it is all of that. Today, however, I am drawn to an implicit part of the story I had never noticed before. C. S. Lewis came to faith "in that room at Magdalen." *Magdalen*. Magdalene. An established, twentieth-century man of faith came to that life in a space whose name associates with one of infamous repute, a woman denied, even denigrated, silenced.

The rebalancing journey I want to invite has a bit of that feel to it—trundling along within well-established, traditional pathways of Christian faith and practice, only to discover a holding-and-being-held within an implicit devotion, ultimately a welcoming Feminine. Finding yourself in a spacious tradition-room presumably conceived and built by men, but at the very last moment, showing *Herself* as the ground, the Ground, upon which or within which all creation, redemption, sanctification . . . the entire path of transfiguration . . . *happens*. Not spiritualized, disembodied, or even glorified, but woundedness transfigured, weakness found strong in the dark of Wisdom, making Light of itself.

There is no posturing in this revelation, no trumpeting of self in hopes of finding Self. No defiant imposition of femininity, feminist righteousness, feminine wisdom. No need—or even patience, perhaps—for masculine guilt and defensiveness. Just a "resurrection of the feminine," a wild tenacity and patience, holding space for human beings to do their work, to awaken to accountability, and to open their hearts to the generative, nourishing, fierce, actively creative energies of the Divine. S/he seems to care little for the names we might use.

C. S. Lewis came to faith within a building of her name and its archetypal energies, devoid of feminine consciousness. My own journey of awakening—with seeds of feminine consciousness planted and now breaking ground into blossoms—resonates, perhaps strangely, with that of C. S.

Lewis. I am not the most reluctant or dejected in this confession and surrender in the Divine, but my eyebrows raise a little and my smile becomes sheepish to name the new reality of a theology professor reborn in the conscious feminine: a Jesus-lovin' devotee of Sacred Mother, claiming lineage within patristic Christianity on a journey of devotion in a way of seeing with the heart. What I have been given? New life in the Feminine, birthing a new Masculine for the common Good.

This One is not in competition with or contradiction to Jesus of Nazareth, the Triune One, or any of the other reigning traditions' g/Gods, but neither is S/he contained within traditional language, habits of mind we've held so tenaciously, to the detriment of so many, both men and women. This One never relinquishes us, no matter how small and insignificant we are, no matter how stubbornly we hold onto conceptions and categories *we* prefer, require, for our allegiance. Ultimately, I've come to know this One deeply through this journey of the heart, unfolded in an excavation of devotion, a path of conscious love received in a return to the body, sacred devotion with companions, sacred touch and holy gaze, in covenantal beholding securely but loosely shaping me in a Love that liberates.

CONCLUSION

Today, now, I see how deep the feminine wound is in our culture, in my own family. I am coming to appreciate how completely terrifying a return to the body and movement into circle-space is for those dissociated and so historically, cognitively defended. For most of the years of this journey, for example, I could not say the word "Goddess" without flinching. Now I can smile into this fear well met, professing that this decade-long pilgrimage has been *of the Goddess*, as Jean Shinoda Bolen describes it: "[A woman's] psyche resides in her body and her wisdom grows out of an instinctual knowledge of what to do with her hands and body to soothe, to comfort, or take charge of a situation that calls upon this in her. . . . When she takes charge by doing whatever needs to be done, Mother has arrived."[2] Again and again in my life, Mother has arrived in the bounded touch of women to bind up what had been bleeding, to release what had been imprisoned in the dark, to nourish the hungers running rampant in my unconscious so that they could nourish others. The start of the journey was an unfortunate manhandling, held in healing care and spiritual friendship. Knowing now

2. Bolen, *Crossing to Avalon*, 70.

what to look for, I can see Mother all the way back to my earliest years. Given the complete predominance of masculine habits of mind and language, I had had little language and few conceptual tools with which to name this experience . . . until now.

So the question arises, how do we hold compassionately yet rigorously those for whom this word, these words of *feminine* and *rebalancing the Divine* and more, instigates reactivity and defense, even violence or condemnation? Nearly every context in which I serve publicly will have little to no felt-sacred context in which to understand my words—the wholeness, atonement, and healing that such words bring. I have been initiated, with a wholehearted willingness that my mind's eye is just coming to see in words. Initiated into my own body, into gifts particular to me and for me to offer, into a life of abundant devotion available to any and all who yearn for it. As I've attempted to demonstrate, this way of coming to Life does not require anyone to relinquish fidelity and wisdom they've been given to know, though it does change you from within. The pathway into the way of the Goddess is a direct result of my Christian faith, rooted in the Incarnation of God in Jesus of Nazareth, whose life, death and (embodied) resurrection have led me to this deeply embodied, compassionate path and abundant devotion. It's time to bring the unconscious and historically driven fears of the Feminine into awareness for both men and women. It's past time.

Circle

The path of devotion in conscious love did not begin in a circle-way community in my own journey. I did not know much about such gatherings, nor how to look for one with what I did know. As the spiritual friendships grew numerous and serial, however, the path inevitably led into relationships with those inclined to gather, listen, and make decisions in a seeker-oriented, nonhierarchical, nonlinear fashion. The circle-way communities of practice in which I now listen deeply to my life manifest what I call the path of devotion in conscious love. The spiritual friendships rooted in conscious love and multiple historic communities/traditions demonstrated energies resonant with those of circle communities. Therefore, this chapter aims to introduce the emotional map and flexible pattern I have experienced both within circle communities of practice and in spiritual friendships that led to a companionable way of being in the world.

One can say "circle," be heard to say "circle," and *still* have failed to communicate what "circle" means, at least in the emotional or archetypal energetic sense I intend. Ecclesial traditions have had "women's circles" for decades, for example, but rarely if ever have I found there the "circle-way energies" I'm trying to describe here. Apples and oranges. Both good fruit, we could say, but I'm just trying to describe one of them. Most times in the circle-way communities of practice I know, we shrug, smile, and say, "You have to be there to experience it for yourself, to receive its wisdom." Some of us have to be in it for as long as a whole semester of circles or a half-year of gatherings to even begin to sense what circle offers those who are hungry for its gifts. Then the question of men and a man's woman arises, because the circle I want to describe has particularly feminine charisms, which men—socialized to dominate and speak out—often struggle to relax in or become *receptive to*. Women socialized into the primacy of men also struggle to receive circling's gifts. I say this bluntly because I have been one of them. Most everyone I know has some unconscious disdain of the feminine. Regardless of definite or fluid gender, some of us take to "circle" with a sense of curiosity and growth, openness to its distinctive gifts. Others do not, and react defensively against the energies circle brings.

Each circle creates a unique signature or charism, co-created and made possible only by those who gather. No less true, there is an archetypal circle-energy or flow that is recognizable in every circle, almost regardless of where or with whom. These descriptions and stories are my own writing the emotional and invitational "map" of this energy or flow as I know it, having been introduced to it with spirit-friends and having participated now in several circle-way communities.

I landed in a circle that felt like Coming Home the evening of March 21, 2012, though I suspect now I'd been preparing—being prepared—for this arrival most of my life. My professional life had long before blossomed in training for peer-group learning, facilitating peer-group curriculum development in various settings, delving into pedagogies of adult transformational learning. A couple of years before 2012, I had been invited into a Red Tent community of women, a circle-way community formed to practice new ways of being in community. This circle prioritizes women's experience and encourages women to return to their bodies, listen deeply to their own intuition, and step into their own life-giving power. We invite speech here, coming to feeling and voice, nonprofessional singing, even "authentic movement" to learn bodyspeak in new ways. Ultimately, we hold space for women's health and healing. The three-four years I had been engaged in such circle practices were shaping my professional life in higher theological education, though I was less conscious of just how much. So, coming into a writing community that fashioned itself to be a circle wasn't inconceivable or unfamiliar. Yet something felt distinct and newly intentional. I couldn't quite name it for a long while, actually. I just knew this learning community was beginning to transform me and my own listening life by leaps and bounds, inside and out.

One way to name it perhaps: these circles are intentional and conscious about being, breathing, and living more deeply into an old-new way of gathering, being present, practicing, making decisions, and more. Each is a circle becoming more and more conscious of itself as a *community* without a hierarchical organization to it. Each circle is organically growing, changing, learning and an interdependent community of practice that gathers and comes into being new each time. The circle in these instances is a community that comes together to be nourished at the center which belongs to no one *and* a community that somehow holds itself loosely enough to receive whomever will enter into it "the next time." The release of "who is in" and "who has not been in" is just as—perhaps more—important than the gatherings themselves.

There is a "movement" or "organizational" component to one of the circle-way communities in which I practice, but we are just as fierce about resisting "decisions of the few" as we are about holding spaces for the gifts in each of us to emerge. We are all familiar with the restrained (or not so restrained) power that has seemed necessary to live in the world today. We see how it has been historically destructive and silencing of so many of us, an "authority" often wielded against the silenced. So the circle gathers for short durations, or at regular intervals, but then releases its energies into the world each time. The circle never knows how it will gather "the next time."

And words are not the only focal point. Silences are just as crucial, perhaps even more so. There is a wordlessness that lives and breathes at the center of these circles. In one, this contemplative Center or wordless heart holds the words of its writers who come to new life and unexpected expression each time the circle gathers. Out of this safety net of silence that allows deeper and deeper presence to self and one another, words emerge that had not been conscious or audible before. In the other circle, this Center holds the music, movement, body wisdom of the women who come to new life and unexpected expression each time the circle gathers. In the Red Tent circle, the spoken and unspoken dance with one another, sometimes figuratively, sometimes literally, breaking open body awareness in women socialized to disregard their own bodies, their own needs. Silence, space, and movement undergird and accompany the wisdom of a circle way.

Red Tent community practices can be glimpsed in a film documentary, *Things We Don't Talk About: Women's Stories from the Red Tent*, created and produced by Isadora Gabrielle Leidenfrost, PhD.[1] The practices of the writing community can be found in the introductory and transformational text authored by Mary Pierce Brosmer, *Women Writing for (a) Change: A Guide for Creative Transformation*. Other circle-way communities teach this energetic way in increasingly available resources—books, videos, conferences, and more: PeerSpirit (Christina Baldwin and Ann Linnea), Circles of Trust (Parker Palmer and Fetzer Institute). *My* words are here simply to invite

---

1. See http://www.redtentmovie.com.

you into the circle energies wherever you live, wherever you may find them. Seek and ye shall find, as the saying goes. I hope you will be encouraged to explore, to enter in deeply wherever you are led, goaded by this glimpse of what many of us have been receiving in such abundance. *But do beware*: when you have your deepest hungers met within a viable circle-way community of practice, your tolerance will decrease steadily for *the way things are* in other communal spaces, even or most especially in traditional communities of practice.

I am still identified within an ecclesial tradition, for instance, but it is painful to sit in "our" gatherings with one person at a time talking at me while most of us are looking at the backs of people's heads. It drives me crazy, actually, so I don't sit there very often anymore. I have learned that the yearning for belonging, the loneliness, fear, self-loathing and turbulence inside each of us can be held, met, transfigured, and released into the world as assurance, self-love, confidence, and abundance. I *know* it in my bones and in my life of companionships. And yet each week, so many of us come to the same old hierarchical structures, so hungry, receiving spoken intimations of this abundance and assurance. Then we head back home, many of us still strangely hungry, yearning, fearful, and more. When you come to *know* in your bones that a life of assurance, abundance, deep change and new life is not only possible but probable within a community that practices awakening and increasing consciousness (inner and communal), it becomes really difficult to remain in the habits of your previous world(s).

You will learn—out of necessity, perhaps—to invite those in your life to join you, but some (many?) will refuse your invitation. Out of their own stories, they will attempt—at best—to convince you that your experience is not legitimate, and at worst to shame or guilt you back into the patterns they have known for so long, which (they believe) *are the tradition*. In a strange, paradoxical way, the only way I know to live into *my* tradition's life-giving invitations has been to relinquish what I have been taught "it is," trusting instead the bodysense of life and love that liberates all shame and fear. Assurance, abundance, devotion, passion, conviction, and more have been the fruit of this way. Not just speaking it, speaking about it, but receiving it in my cells, in my very being. The conscious world *becomes* abundance, devotion, passion, conviction—experienced and incontrovertible—without denying the radical evil, suffering, and more that are *in* this world. You come to *know* the pearl of great price. The field for which you would sell everything you own. And you learn to know it for longer and longer periods of time amidst the same old mental and communal snares that will refine your knowing.

PATTERN AND FLOW

The circle-way communities I know follow a predictable flow each gathering, though each circle gathering differs too. The basic parts of this flow are:

1. Finding—Entering
2. Opening (Creating Container)
3. Becoming Present (Check-In, etc.)
4. Tending (Arc of Gathering) and Going Deeper (Fastwrite; Guided Meditation)
5. Practice (Sharing Words, Naming Intentions, Card-Making)
6. Re-connecting/Mixing (Break; Shifting Energies, Re-checking-In)
7. Tending (Completion of Arc)
8. Closing (Releasing Container Intention, Energies; Preparation to Return to the World)

In this flow, I have learned many things, as elemental as how to welcome people into a this new-ancient way, how to listen more deeply than I knew possible, how to become deeply present. I have been returned to the power of the spoken word as event, to describe it in the language of an ecclesial tradition that has held me. I have also been shown the necessity and immediacy of *contemporary* voices, grounded in their own experience and less constrained by "authoritative sacred tradition." (Our sacred traditions always condition how we come to voice, whether they are contemporary streams of practice or recognized historical traditions.) I've begun to learn how to describe "circle" from my own experience of it, as invitation, as testimony, as teaching. I will share here from my first entrance point, reflecting what rises as significant for broad attention, whether you identify within a tradition or are seeking a community within which to belong just as you are.

Finding—Entering

Each of us lands in circle in a way organic to our own story, our own choices. I had had a bad day at work. Someone said something at a faculty meeting that enraged me. I don't even remember what it was anymore, but it hit a deep rawness in me about being a woman in theological education. I drove home, stomped upstairs to my writing desk, opened the computer. Into the Google search engine—Oracle Google, in this case—I pounded "women" and "writing," two words that seemed to encapsulate what my soul-body needed at that moment. A safe community of women and a place I could delve deeply into what *did* feed me, which was my writing. Up came a link for a nontraditional writing school. I startled to learn it was less than an hour away from me. I delighted to see a new eight-week class was beginning in about three weeks. I signed up on the spot, and three weeks later entered into an upstairs open space of a writing hall, about twenty chairs in a circle. In the center of the circle was a vase of cut flowers, resting on a circle cloth, and soft music was playing from a CD player close to the facilitator's chair. Women were arriving one by one, some sitting in a chair in the circle, others gathering quietly in the kitchen over light refreshments. I sat down in one of the chairs to gather my thoughts and calm my nervous energies. As the music played, I began to quiet, to center, to truly *arrive*, and then a chime sounded. I had entered this circle community of practice.

Opening

I learned the importance of a chime that night, for opening, for startling, for clearing a space, for closing. There's something about a bell that, just for a moment, creates a slightly different space and time of attention, intention. A chime differs from a whistle, for instance, blown by my college soccer coach to gather us from across the field. It differs from a school bell, loud and programmed to ring on the hour. A chime—usually a Tibetan singing bowl, in this case—opens a space with clear intention but also a softness of spirit. The sound startles too, sometimes because your body-mind wasn't ready for it or expecting it. Sometimes because you become aware of the noisiness in your own mind as it focuses on the sound, relinquishing itself into silence. In any case, this circle uses the chime to clear a space for intention, for listening anew to women's words, for signaling a gentle end to spoken words.

Next, the lighting of a candle in a bowl and passing it around the circle in silence creates a ritual space of intention, invitation, and receptivity. We call this "creating a container for our words," but it could create such a space for whatever the circle intention might be. When each circle gathers, after the chime rings, the facilitator lights a candle, placed in a small bowl, often with beautiful stones surrounding it. After a time of silent holding it herself, perhaps listening for an intention, she passes it to the person next to her. Each person in the circle holds it just long enough for the flame to still, for the silent intention to arise, before passing it to the next person. The flame reflects on the face of the beholder, signaling a spark within, the light within, held with intention, shared in gentle offering, gentle receiving. From the very beginning, a ritual practice of giving, holding, and receiving has been enacted in a spacious quiet for each, for all. In this participation, each who has held the candle silently signals agreement to the intentional space and an invitation to create a "container" to hold the words and energies of all those present.

Some folks entering into this *opening* struggle with the associations and feelings that can arise. For some, it feels "too Catholic," this lighting of a candle and creation of intentional space, "set apart for particular purpose." Many who find their way into circle-way communities have deep wounds from historic-contemporary religious communities, Roman Catholic being one of them. Others find the extended silence disconcerting, now accustomed to the hustle and bustle of overworked North American culture(s). Inner noise to which they are unaccustomed arises in the quiet, and no skills or awareness have been shaped in them to know how to hold the noise in mind or body. The community as a whole, however, recognizes the crucial importance of the ritual opening. It provides a predictable, participatory practice within which folks may become present with one another, within which communal intention for co-creation, receiving, and offering may take shape again and again. Myself, I like that my body learns the *feeling* of receiving, being-seen, and then offering. This creates a gentle, safe space for whatever practice comes next.

A quote and poem chosen by the facilitator are read at each gathering of this circle community, which has taught me the expected yet unpredictable power of the spoken word and the pressing immediacy of contemporary voices naming their own experience. As an ecclesial leader, I have been trained in and have participated in the practice of spoken word for years. Traditional communities have been entirely shaped around it, after all, in some fashion: scripture read and interpreted, liturgical words of ritual actions repeated again and again. If you come from a traditional community of some religious or philosophical persuasion, this reading of a poem might resonate in that way. But there are more differences than similarities, in my experience here, in what I've learned.

For one thing, there is no particular "canon" or "authoritative source" of the poetry to begin a circle. The facilitator chooses it as led by desire, intuition, or as the creative spark invites. Choices could be determined by the day, the place, the people gathered, a topic of interest, a need, etc. What is required is that the poem be readable, able to become *spoken word*. Some poems, particularly by classical voices of high literate traditions, are simply not readable in oral fashion today. Too wordy, or too dense. Archaic language and inaccessible contexts. So the circle comes to life in an event of spoken word most often in contemporary voice.

What stunned me was the immediate invitation into *my own experience* when hearing contemporary voices, *naming their own experience* in a fashion well suited to the ears in the circle. Perhaps it *is* my familiarity with spoken word taken largely from ancient texts that predisposes me to hear spoken word in a certain way, but the "holy ordinary" of contemporary poetry burst open a doorway to my own experience in a way sacred scripture has not, or can no longer, for a variety of reasons. Hearing the words of men and women staying close to their own observations, fears, wonderings, wrestlings within the human experience? Very little has goaded me as much as this has—to listen more deeply, to question more gently, to find more compassion in myself for the silences with me and those around me.

All of which has, oddly, returned me to the deep roots of my own ecclesial tradition—the necessity of word as *event*—and mirrored to me how far this "tradition" has strayed from its roots of *word for the people there*. The word read and interpreted in ecclesial/religious traditions I have participated in today has such historical remove, such inaccessible authority "out there," needing to be interpreted by the one "up there." Even as leadership tries to persuade otherwise, it proclaims a Sacred held at some remove from those receiving it. Participation can become abstract, removed, disembodied. From the circle, deeply resonant with my own tradition, I have learned how a community can come to life around word as event, and how it can foment deep inner work if the words arise through immediately available, contemporary voices.

An entirely "new" old stage has now been set, in a circle created in an opening just like this. A community has gathered into intention, invitation, shared silence and spoken word. Each has been seen in the passing of the candle, which means participation has been ritually established, regardless of skill, social location, or voice. Everyone is, by definition, a participant and co-creator of the space that rests in the circle.

Becoming Present (Check-In, etc.)

After the circle opens, a talking piece is traditionally passed around with invitation to "check in" and bring yourself present in words, or a welcome that could be a chosen silence. One circle insists on each woman stating her first name each time the stone comes to her. Women have few enough opportunities to *name themselves* that this is what this circle invites. Another circle doesn't always use a talking piece or stating one's name, but invites each person to check in as welcome. When the speaker is truly finished, she will put both hands on the floor or table to signal she has said what she needed to say. In either case, the invitation is for each circle member to come to voice, be heard in that voice, choose to share "whatever will bring her most present" into that time and place.

Sometimes the writing circle will begin this process by "echoing a line" from the poem read. This honors the poet's voice and connects each person's experience with whatever was read. It also serves as a gentle bridge from the "words of another" into "one's own words." By the time the talking piece has traveled the circle, or each woman has spoken and placed her hands on the table or floor, the circle community has had opportunity to become aware, or at least open to, collectively, the most pressing emotional-physical-spiritual energies in the room. Depending on the size of the circle, of course, the check-ins are necessarily brief, suggestive, evocative. Each person learns how to honor his/her own voice while honoring the boundaries necessary for *all* voices to be heard. The facilitator can step in if one member begins to "hold court" without realizing the imbalance he or she is creating.

Tending (Arc of Gathering) and Going Deeper (Fastwrite; Guided Meditation)

Each circle gathering, a short time is taken for "tending the arc of the circle," or welcoming folks into conscious expectations of the time together. One circle does this with the agenda that is crafted and printed for each member. Another does this with the "grandmother" of the circle reminding the whole gathering of shared space and personal intentions for each to care for herself, listen to her body, do what she needs to do while being attentive to the flow of the whole. This is probably the most directive or "public leadership" moment in the circle so far, allowing those who are "holding the space" to empower members to be attentive to self and other and to ease any anxieties about whatever invitations are coming in the circle process. Empowerment and ease, both. For the circle with the printed agenda, the facilitator or circle-holder will just highlight the major elements of the time together, using few words but enough to welcome everyone into a sense of expectation and ability to contribute as much as possible.

All of this has then prepared the circle for a time of deepening, a practice of some sort that weaves the energies of those present into a shared endeavor of listening, writing, envisioning, etc. In the Red Tent circle community, we often enter into a guided meditation together, offered by one of the women who has been to many circles before. In this context, there is invitation to attend to the breath, to become more aware of one's own body-stories and sensations. How do we bring the mind into the heart, the heart deeper into the core energies of the body? How does awareness expand if we allow more of us to become present, speak, communicate? When I stop, breathe, and listen to the body, I often find that it is shouting at me. So much of my work and my life has been centered in the intellect, in the head, that I often struggle to return to the body, to listen deeply into what my muscles, tissues, cells may be screaming at me while I attend elsewhere. When I become present in the breath, in this way, I contact a deep source of implicit information, even intuition and awarenesses that have guided me well over the years. I am regularly in awe that I constantly forget the wealth of resources there for me. I wind up "rediscovering it" again and again, usually with frustration that I don't just *live* from there.

In the writing circle, our practice of deepening is a time of fastwriting together. Springboarding from a prompt, a line from the poem or quote, or something from the day that draws attention, each member writes for ten to fifteen minutes. The circle grows quiet, the sound of pens and pencils can be heard, sometimes the click-clack of a computer keyboard from the next room (often a practice of those who don't want to disturb the organic with the technological). Sometimes the flow comes easily and a writer will find a gem of reflection s/he had been unaware of before. Sometimes this is a painful time of awareness that the mind and heart are too busy, too full, to find the slow pace of handwriting a comfortable invitation. Either way, the writers become more aware of their own words, associations, presence (or overbusyness), and the circle as a whole deepens its energy of presence for all those there.

Practice (Sharing Words, Naming Intentions, Card-Making)

Circles gather for countless reasons. The ones in focus here name particular purposes, such as writing or New Moon gathering, but in my life, both have aimed at deepening my listening life and inviting the inner work necessary to encounter an "other" peaceably. The professed mission of Women Writing for (a) Change is *to nurture and celebrate the individual voice by facilitating supportive writing circles and by encouraging people to craft more conscious lives through the art of writing and the practices of community.* Seen from the outside, the practice looks like "just writing." Women gather here to learn how to write, to deepen their writing, even to push their writing into the world. All of that does and may happen. But this circle-way community lives and breathes through writing *in community*, so it entails a complex and widely expressive *combination of practices* in some contrast to a reductionistic assumption of "just writing."

A wide variety of values and actions are necessary to nurture and celebrate the individual voice, after all. The first value named is *community*. In contrast to the notion of writing as a primarily literate activity, this circle community conceives of writing as an individual voice being offered and received in a deeply listening community. "Writing does not exist in a vacuum," observes Mary Pierce Brosmer, the founder. "It exists in a reciprocal relationship with others—those who hear and respond to the words sent out." As such, the circle hones skills in becoming present, being accountable to creative disciplines, conscious attention, deep listening, and more. Reverence for creative expression and shared time go hand in hand. *Joy* and *respect* create open spaces for the expression of voices in words and silences. The community takes pleasure in the beauty of words, the intimacy in silence, the joy in the acts of creating. Safe spaces are required for this to blossom, so both openness and healthy boundaries are regularly created and evaluated. *Mentoring* and *connection* undergird the community as well. This circle community has grown through intergenerational participation, with elders mentoring youth and youth leading elders. When the individual voice is nurtured, this kind of exchange happens with great frequency. Most of all, *hospitality* courses through the creation and release of these circles in the nearly twenty-five-year history of the community. Precise attention to details provides a welcome often felt more than seen.

The vision within which this mission unfolds is *to bring the feminine more fully into expression by supporting the voices and stories of girls and women of all races, classes, and nations*. Again, the stated practice of this circle is writing, but writing that brings women and girls to words, and their words to the world (tagline for a radio show the community did for a while). Given the often hostile climate for women in the world, at least for women being true to themselves first, this practice of writing requires a whole combination of practices for the community that can and will support women *writing*.

The conscious intention *to bring the feminine more fully into expression* undergirds the other circle-way community in which I have grown, contributed, deepened. Red Tent circles—a grass-roots movement, of sorts, happening across the country—gather by means of a variety of practices as well. Moon cycles determine the rhythm of gatherings—New Moon, Full Moon, Solstice gatherings, for instance. New Moon gatherings are for each woman to name an intention for herself for the month. Full Moon gatherings are more raucous, celebratory of the intentions coming to fruition or the journey toward that end. At the heart of this ebb-and-flow community, however, is *practicing new ways for women to awaken and claim their own wholeness*, in the community of women. There is *being-time*, which is simply unstructured and open-ended time for women to arrive at the circle-space and share in food, welcoming rituals, conversation, storytelling, and more. When the circle opens, the practice is one of speaking-listening-singing and more. Each woman retrieves a "talking piece" from the center of the circle and names briefly her intention, whatever words she wants to speak into the listening community, holding her in gentle focus and care. The invitation is repeated again and again—to learn how to care for oneself while also holding loving care for each other.

As this section began, so it concludes: circles gather for countless reasons, some focused on a particular practice and others more diffusely structured with a broader goal of relearning community, how to be anew in community that goads you to wholeness. Civic communities will sometimes gather in circle now to make decisions about shared resources. Schools are finding the value of circle-way learning, integrating its archetypal energies into processes to accomplish specific learning objectives. One art form I've learned recently—SoulCollage—is also a combination of practices integrated into the Women Writing for (a) Change circle-way. As each circle gathers, then, some practice or focus shapes the individual and communal voice.

Re-connecting/Mixing (Break; Shifting Energies, Re-checking-In)

Each circle also has a balance of formal and informal space, necessary to allow the safety or comfort of structure *and* invite a spontaneous or surprising shift in the energies coming together. In one circle, this "informal" gift comes largely at the beginning—being-time, we call it—but ripples throughout the rest of the formal time in the persistent invitation to *care for yourself, listen to your body, tend to what you need in this place.* Even be willing *to ask for what you need*, in this place, without any self-judgment or communal disdain usually called "selfish" or "self-centered." No. In this circle, to know what you want or need and to be willing to ask for it shows a self-knowledge and courage particularly important for women (or those in the helping professions, perhaps, trained to put the needs of others *always* before their own). It's the imbalance that is unhealthy or destructive of truly intimate community, not the self's ability to name what she needs in balance with the "we" that is present. Women tending to themselves, being accountable to their own needs, offers the spontaneous and rippling flow throughout the formal circle time.

In another community, this time of mixing or reconnecting happens with a break for refreshments before the large circle regathers. Perhaps someone brought savory or sweet treats to share. Or the pot of coffee and hot water for tea draw those there into a new movement of persons and voices. In any case, a break offers opportunity to connect with folks you haven't spoken with directly for a while, to meet newer members of the circle, to be in the space in some new ways unstructured by formal circle time.

Tending (Completion of Arc—Soul Cards)

The writing circle begins to draw its energies to a close with a "tending" practice we call "soul cards." The simple act of writing gifts/challenges onto an index card at the close of a circle, this practice *tends* the conscious and unconscious lives of those who have gathered. Read at the start of the next circle gathering—or left in the basket there for anyone to read, as she chooses—these cards name the gifts people actually experienced, in their own words. They describe personal and sometimes communal challenges experienced too—a time when feelings were hurt, or something was said that made another defensive. Anonymous but present, these words help the circle become conscious of itself, of how it is being held, of how it is co-creating a safe—or not as safe—container for each to be herself in a community of others. The readings are also not to fix or problem-solve anything that is read aloud. Simply a telling, a witness, which—counterintuitively—allows the circle to trust that the celebratory and difficult energies *will be tended* in the intentions and care of the whole. The circle-holder is not responsible, ultimately, but the circle is. The leader is not told and then expected to address it; the circle is told, and expected to learn from it. Truth-telling, individual accountability, and communal trust become the fruit of the practice over time.

Closing (Releasing Container, Energies; Preparation to Return to the World)

One of the most recent awarenesses for me is the importance of the closing, perhaps even more important than the finding and gathering itself. As the agreed-upon time of conclusion draws near, each circle begins to move collectively toward a closure of some kind. One circle moves in close, being able to share physical space in hands touching, arms holding each person in the weave of the circle. Sitting or standing there in an active silence, the circle-holder will often invite a song to come, from anyone who feels it bubbling up. The group will join in if we know it, or hum along if we don't. It need not be sung well to serve its purpose of thanksgiving, connection, and closing. Another circle retrieves the lit candle from the center space, passing it back around to each woman, signaling the shared intention to release each who had been present back into the energies of the world at large. A chime is rung when the extinguished candle is placed back at the center.

Song, passing the candle, sound—each ritual element communicates to the bodies present that the focused intentions and practices have concluded. There is a definite ending and those gathered are free to move back into their "other" spaces without energetic tie or sense of obligation. No one knows whether the circle that gathers next time will have the same people or similar energies as the previous one. Even in the core-circle community that commits to being present for, say, a period of fifteen weeks, people's lives are such that the precise constitution of the circle can change from week to week. So there is a balance of sustained presence and freedom to choose whether or not to be present "next time." In a strange way, the release is crucial for the return to have its liberating welcome.

CONCLUDING OBSERVATIONS

For those who find their voices within a circle-way community, it can be difficult to understand how such abundance can be resisted, or why such hospitable gathering could be undesirable. While circle-way gatherings live into equity and a commitment to each person present, they are not for everyone, even within a companionable way. Given how many of us have been conditioned to be in community—socialized in schooling models of education or in hierarchical models of religious traditions—the fact of co-creation and participation can simply be unnerving. Circles gather and each person is seen, possibly *deeply* seen. There is very little anonymity, though silence and presence are not only welcome but necessary. For those accustomed to being in a crowd, hiding among those who speak out more readily, circle-way community can simply be too intimate, too vulnerable.

Additionally, speaking in any kind of gathering, for many of us, means *public speaking* or *leadership*, which requires preparation, training, and particular skills determined by others. The possibility of appearing or feeling foolish, incompetent, or unprepared brings huge pressure to those of us who hear or feel a demand or expectation in *participation*. Who wants to be heard or seen "in public" when you don't know what you are going to say or how you are supposed to be? Therefore, stress, fear, and anxiety can arise.

For many shaped in traditional or ecclesial communities, whether that shaping has been life-affirming or not, another even more damning question arises: how do you relax while being seen in a circle space with others when you've been told, implicitly or explicitly, that what is within you is sinful, shameful, and guilt-ridden? For those within Christian habits of mind, this demeaning of the body and belief in sin or depravity can prevent self-acceptance, or worse, lead to self-loathing. Who wants to become visible while mired in self-loathing? Circle spaces for those of us so mired bring fear, shame, and more.

Circle ways also bring a disruptive equity into age-old assumptions about power, voice, and leadership. Having begun to explore circle-way leadership within the contexts of higher education, I have learned that such practices of community can be both consciously and unconsciously resisted. Socialized practices of speaking and being heard in these contexts rest upon a certain vocal aggression, even what has been called "conceptual violence" of speech, critical rebuttal, revision. Those who have learned to *get heard* in critical discourse can find the created-space for *all* voices, each with equal measure, unnerving. The skill set honed in academic formation becomes a liability to the whole. Receptivity and vulnerability within academic formation are not highly valued, so rarely practiced or rewarded. On the other hand, those who have been silenced in habits of discourse—those who you would assume would warm immediately to the hospitable welcome of their voices—do not easily trust the circle is really as open and welcoming as it is. It is too vulnerable a space to take the chance of being silenced again, this time in public, in front of everyone there.

Even when each person elects the kind of participation that is comfortable—speaking or remaining silent, or speaking very little, only slowly speaking more—it remains exceedingly difficult to trust that the generosity and equanimity of the circle really *is* as generous and welcoming as it professes to be. In every conscious circle into which I have been welcomed, everyone's way of being in that space is by invitation, not obligation. You are responsible for your own well-being *and* for balancing the "me" and the "we" in the presence of others who are likewise responsible for *them*selves. It does take practice, of course. It is hard to learn and come to trust, steeped in distrust and learned hatreds as we are, but the circle is co-created by all who gather. Each has a vested interest in being an advocate for oneself and an "other," while holding the tensions that sometimes requires.

Invitation, not obligation. Presume good will. These two phrases serve as a cornerstone practice for whatever unfolds next in the circle energies I describe here. Human beings are always works in progress, which means things will happen in this circle space that both assure and challenge, affirm and refute those I hold dear. No one else in the circle is just like me—thank heaven—and I am unlike anyone else in the circle. What I have come to know as true, right, and good may or may not resonate with the convictions, stories, and actions of another. These two phrases, held in regular commitment and practice, create a space where very different human beings may yet sit in circle, in community, together—each responsible for him/herself, each practicing openness to the other.

Invitation, not obligation holds open an inward-listening space for my life unlike most other spaces that are in my life. Sitting there, I can listen for what is calling for my attention, not demanding some response. I learn to hear how much choice I actually *do* have in my life, how much life *is* an invitation to more, not a duty or list of "shoulds" imposed upon me by others. What it means in practice is "welcome just as you are," and "we mean it." "Our circle life does not require you to spend more of yourself than you can or do things that are not healthy for you to do." "Our best Self stems from each of us learning to offer our best selves, step by step, moment to moment." "What is good for all of us must be gleaned and grow from what is good for each of us, in the presence of all of us." This kind of profession is impossible within a *scarcity* mindset, by the way. It can only arise as conceivable if you are willing to practice abundance, look for the whole, imagine the betterment in each and all. Which, given what we see in the news, is and always must be *a practice*.

Presume good will holds the same force, often even greater need for practice, as this one focuses outward to those whose words or actions may impact you negatively. When something upsetting or surprising happens in civic life today, something that instigates strong emotion, even a defensive reaction, what is the learned response for most of us? Defend what we have known, sometimes in words? React in the overflow of emotion, perhaps—pouring our outrage or ire into political channels or lines of gossip in our social relationships? Fight or flight, some describe it. We are affirmed for political advocacy, funded by anger or rage (fight), or we withdraw to the private realms of our lives, where we can find the most security, even affirmation, for what we know or how we live. The practice of *presume good will* offers a middle way, in a communal structure where each is responsible for his/her own words and actions in a practiced balance of me/we. This phrase encourages each to sit with whatever arises, held within the energies of the circle, learning to trust, honor, and give each participant the benefit of the doubt for showing up to be present, to be vulnerable, to offer as well as to receive. If each is entering into the invitation, after all, what is being offered has a freedom and an integrity for wherever that person is in her or his journey, coming to awareness about what matters. *Presume good will* is a practice of honoring.

So where do we go from here? Perhaps unhelpful, but none of us has a viable, overarching plan to offer you. The Dalai Lama's quip comforts and confounds: "Although attempting to bring about world peace through the internal transformation of individuals is difficult, it is the only way."[2] The statement—*the internal transformation of individuals*—points to a messy, unpredictable, long-term, intimate path with few ready-made patterns fit for all. Perhaps disorienting for many of us, the way of companionship tendered here offers little to no standardization, and certainly not a one-fits-many approach. *Individuals*, he says. "One at a time." And "it is the only way."

Parker Palmer observes this, too, in a brief piece on community.[3] Community needs to be expansive enough to include strangers, coworkers, civic/local neighbors. Our need for intimacy—for being seen, heard, enough just as we are—both will and *will not* be met in "community." He *does* urge for "pockets of possibility" within today's hierarchical and rapidly changing institutions. Circle-way leadership learning strikes me as a particularly potent "pocket of possibility" within today's organizational bodies. No less true, circle-way webs of belonging need development and support *outside* of today's institutional landscapes, ecologies. Circle-way communities need to be viably independent of current structures *and* related to them, with compassion, energy, and insight. The transformation of this individual would never have been possible within the institutions I still serve. What made it possible were two circle communities of women, independent, fiercely gentle with me, culturally courageous and bold.

---

2. The Dalai Lama, cited in May, "From Cruelty to Compassion," 165.

3. Palmer, "Thirteen Ways of Looking at Community ... with a Fourteenth Thrown in for Free."

Conclusion

Attempting to invite participation and reflection on a companionable way of being in the world by means of a book is, perhaps, the height of foolishness and implausibility. I love books. I need books. I need the anticipation of connection, information, and suggestion that they bring to my life. But I now know I need the overt audience or visible and responsive presence "on the other side" of words shared aloud and in community that books simply do not assure. There is a potentially volatile, even dissociated space that solely printed, literate expression creates that face-to-face, oral-audible sharing of words closes, protected within the sanctuary of a circle. I'm reminded of a favorite William Stafford poem, "A Ritual to Read to Each Other," naming the importance of truly *seeing* one another, knowing *other-wise,* as we are led. When we refuse to see what-is, the literate habits of years can determine our actions. We miss our giftedness, our potential.[1] Books reveal a lot of things, but they also conceal the body language of a soul, the energetic signatures we carry, the intuitive-implicit-inarticulate truths of who we are. Sometimes books conceal that from our very selves as we focus on the words to understand our experience and allow the sensate world and its communications to atrophy. We don't know "others" often because we have not delved into the inner work of knowing ourselves. We don't know the kind of people we are, and patterns that others have made *do* prevail. We are missing our star.

It has been my task, my own sense of urgency, to point to a path of devotion in conscious love made possible when you enter into a willingness presented you, an embodied heart-seeing way of awakening to and encountering others. I named this willingness in several stories of choiceless choice in which it took root in me: a willingness to be grounded in

---

1. Stafford, "A Ritual to Read to Each Other," in *Stories That Could Be True.*

exile, to find deep roots in difference, to sense belief in unexpected places of nontheism, to know faith deeply amidst the fear of betrayal, to befriend and be befriended by outsiders, to be rebirthed and initiated into the sacred in new-old ways. The yearnings that drive us today are infinitely diverse and yet consistent and predictable too: safety, love, belonging, purpose, connection in worth offered outwardly. The habits of mind we cultivate determine so much of what we experience, if not all that comes at us.

What is required is awakening to holy desire to encounter an "other," with vulnerability and willingness to be changed *from within* by that encounter. This is *hard* inner work that requires learning to *see with the heart*, conceiving of knowledge in a fashion "wise to the other" in addition to the objectivist, dispassioned senses of knowledge that reign today. While inundated with linguistically aggressive and polarized habits of mind, we then may practice *both/and* consciousness—dualistic or polarized dialectics *and* primarily relational, deeply embodied knowing that unifies. This practice requires constant listening, sensing, for third-ways, unexpected *both/and* possibilities not immediately visible to the eye but drawn forward by embodied heart awareness. Amidst dialogue and conceptual attempts to build bridges between traditions, political persuasions, and more, the path of devotion in conscious love beckons for any and all weary of the now predictable debates. Within this river flow, you find yourself in belief amidst nontheists and faithful in all fears of betrayal. You find yourself befriended as an outsider, and befriending outsiders; strangers become companions. The consciousness able to hold such things for prolonged periods of time is what I name a new-old sacred, the conscious feminine in a holy dance with a new conscious masculine. The Feminine finds priority here, if only because so few of us can sustain Her receptive wordlessness and grounding energy that unifies without power, loves without attachment, opens without expectation of return. At least as much as each of us can withstand it and learn to practice this in body.

In my little corner of the world, I'm eager for the cognitive aggression and socialized disdain of higher education (both within it and imposed upon it) to soften, even diffuse, into a more supple means of connecting through bounded deep feeling and stronger communal containers—both able to hold critical discourse in a way that it refines rather than consumes, warms rather than destroys. I have been overwhelmingly blessed to find—or to be found in—the "pockets of possibility"[2] I have, the circle-way com-

2. Palmer, "Thirteen Ways of Looking at Community."

munities that see and hear me deeply, allowing me to practice heart-seeing and deep listening with others. I would not know what I know without them, without the spirit-friends who have risked so much to learn with me, to love me and receive my love.

That said, this book has changed me. It has transfigured my inner and outer life toward a sacred wholeness I never knew possible, which means it has been as *costly* as it is compelling (for me). By and large, people do not like change. Or at least change that they haven't directed or selected themselves. Made conscious, articulated well, the disorientation that change brings can be held with compassion in marriages, families, today's communities, and more. This is change within reason. Improvement of what-already-is with the side effect of satisfaction that what-is can offer precisely what we hope will be, what is required for health, wholeness, and the pursuit of happiness for all. Mutual awakening unfolds, then, opening companions to deeper and broader consciousness that weaves opposites into unities until one-ness is the lens through which you both can see the world—first and perhaps forever, for only moments at a time. A deeper conundrum awaits, however, with the level of internal and structural change instigated in the path of devotion in conscious love in spiritual friendships or in circle-way communities.

Deeply renewing wholeness found outside of—even if alongside—traditional pathways, traditional structures, can *threaten* those we love, those who love us. The social force of the belonging you've always known can be so very strong, even if it disconnects you from your deepest self, your own embodied wisdom. I didn't *know* my own capacity, nor that life could be as rich and abundant as I now know it *can* be. Those who have found some semblance of peace and security in *the way things are* will not be eased by your new ways of being, *new possibilities of doing* with which they are *unfamiliar*. In a strange way, then, the peace and security found in a wholeness deeply rooted within, held in webs of companions "beyond," creates a sacred, refining fire, even a "sword" that cuts through illusion. It is costly and painful, even as it is more compelling and abundant than anything I have ever known. An assurance and abundance emerge almost without thought, steadying and balancing you amidst these changes, while conflict and fear may arise with those you love. This kind of change is that *beyond* reason, that within the rationality a conscious love knows—in reduced reciprocity, insufficient reason, and deep-bones insight and awareness. Love proves to offer the most promising yet volatile and unpredictable kind of change. The only way it can be sustained for any period of time is if a strong enough container holds you while the ripple effect of your own journey courses through your life.

The focal point of this entire invitational, interactive, intuitive text has been the need to awaken to the unconscious burden and conscious gift that deep feeling can be for human being toward an expressive delight able to companion the suffering of self and others. The best of life I have been privileged to know can hold the worst, if shared within a community-container able to hold a whole greater than its parts. The deep pains of human life I have known—such as they are in my life of privilege—can refine and be refined in conscious love, flowing in and beyond a spiritual companionship with one(s) willing to go deep and hold onto you as the devotion transfigures whatever needs refinement. The "containers" in which I have lived most of my life are beautiful, holy ones simply unable to hold all that the world is pouring into them today. They do not become unholy or "bad," yet the path of devotion in conscious love beckons me into the silences, into the friendships and containers that *can* hold deep feeling as the *gift* it is.

The way I have been shown to delve into this burden, now gift, of deep feeling is one of spiritual friendship and circle-way communities currently independent of more traditional kinds of communities (religious tradition, political, etc.). The challenge of staying connected and comprehensible within traditional structures *has* been a difficult stretch as these words move a companionable way out into more public conversations. I have struggled to keep a foot in each boat, wondering how long I can. *As long as thou canst*, came the historical Quaker answer. For now, the sense of connection to the Sacred rises for me within those hearts hungry and listening within traditional structures as well as within the hearts of those hungry and listening outside my own faith community, outside what we might call "traditional structures" of any kind. To be clear, I have also felt the absence of the Sacred within and outside of traditional structures, a coldness and spirit-searing sensation of absence, limitation, void. I nod to the evidence of radical evil, radical suffering in the world, without words or answers. I have slammed into my own limitations, my own finite capacities, having to learn how to steward my own smallness within a world more mysterious, inviting, and awe-somely terrifying than I can withstand.

The task as I have been shaped in these years has been to enter in where I am welcome—sacred spaces, spiritual practices, challenging conversations and encounters—and sense deeply and quietly within my own

Conclusion

body, my own sensate awarenesses that rise. This way is not for everyone, surely, but I have found it to be revelatory, insightful, and wondrous beyond anything I could imagine. Walt Whitman's imperative names my current aim to live whatever years remain to me, with a quiet discernment and companionable integrity: "Re-examine all you have been told at school or church or in any book, dismiss whatever insults your own soul, and your very flesh shall be a great poem and have the richest fluency not only in its words but in the silent lines of its lips and face and between the lashes of your eyes and in every motion and joint of your body."[3]

When rooted in spiritual companionships across multiple traditions, when holding and being held within the circle-energies of practice communities, you can live this flow of devotion within institutions and religious traditions purported to be declining, dying. You can live this flow of devotion on the very peripheries of current communities, adding your leaven to the whole, as your body leads. Your wisdom may be welcomed, in which case you follow the streams of welcome. What you have to say, how you are being shown to live into what you encounter, may be denied, resisted, even profaned. When rooted in spiritual companionships across multiple traditions, when holding-and-being-held within circle-way communities, however, most of that begins to matter less. You find yourself strengthened more and more, deeply Rooted in the Sacred regardless of location or impositions. You begin to find the Sacred available to you deep within your bodysoul, which is posited in the Spirit whose energies brought you into the world in the first place. I dare say this is how change has always happened within streams of living tradition—pockets of possibility that hold new ways of being human together amidst the structures that worked years/centuries ago. What I had never sensed so deeply is how abundant and life-giving a difficult path of change would be, but how *else* could new life emerge?

Drawn forward by that which is sought, perhaps a way of companionship already unfolding can come into greater awareness, new stories and beautiful words of both light and shadow. For myself, it has required a return to the body, a path of devotion in conscious love across difference, and a trusting in the quiet holy dark forgotten in fear. My prayer is that I may rest and work in this living, breathing center with those who are willing to come alongside, remain, and push us all forward in faith.

---

3. Whitman, *Leaves of Grass*, 11.

Bibliography

Baldwin, Christina. *Calling the Circle: The First and Future Culture.* New York: Bantam, 1998.

———. *The Seven Whispers: Listening to the Voice of Spirit.* Novato, CA: New World Library, 2002.

Baldwin, Christina, and Ann Linnea. *The Circle Way: A Leader in Every Chair.* San Francisco: Berrett-Koehler, 2010.

Bolen, Jean Shinoda. *Crossing to Avalon: A Woman's Midlife Quest for the Sacred Feminine.* San Francisco: HarperSanFrancisco, 1994.

———. *The Millionth Circle: How to Change Ourselves and the World.* The Essential Guide to Women's Circles. Berkeley: Conari, 1999.

Bourgeault, Cynthia. *The Holy Trinity and the Law of Three: Discovering the Radical Truth at the Heart of Christianity.* Boston: Shambhala, 2013.

———. *Love Is Stronger than Death: The Mystical Union of Two Souls.* New York: Bell Tower, 1999.

———. *The Meaning of Mary Magdalene: Discovering the Woman at the Heart of Christianity.* Boston: Shambhala, 2010.

———. *The Wisdom Way of Knowing: Reclaiming an Ancient Tradition to Awaken the Heart.* San Francisco: Jossey-Bass, 2003.

Bradbury, Ray. *Fahrenheit 451.* New York: Simon & Schuster, 2003.

Brosmer, Mary Pierce. *Women Writing for (a) Change: A Guide for Creative Transformation.* Notre Dame: Sorin, 2009.

Brown, Brené. "The Power of Vulnerability." June 2010. http://www.ted.com/talks/brene_brown_on_vulnerability?language=en.

Cameron, Julia. *The Artist's Way: A Spiritual Path to Higher Creativity.* 10th anniversary ed. New York: Jeremy P. Tarcher/Putnam, 2002.

Carnes, Robin Deen, and Sally Craig. *Sacred Circles: A Guide to Creating Your Own Women's Spirituality Group.* San Francisco: HarperSanFrancisco, 1998.

Chittister, Joan. *Welcome to the Wisdom of the World and Its Meaning for You.* Grand Rapids: Eerdmans, 2007.

Chittister, Joan, Saadi Shakur Chishti, and Arthur Waskow. *The Tent of Abraham: Stories of Hope and Peace for Jews, Christians, and Muslims.* Boston: Beacon, 2006.

Duerk, Judith. *Circle of Stones: Woman's Journey to Herself.* 10th anniversary ed. Philadelphia: Innisfree, 1999.

Eck, Diana. *A New Religious America: How a "Christian Country" Has Become the World's Most Religiously Diverse Nation.* San Francisco: HarperSanFrancisco, 2002.

Bibliography

Edwards, Tilden. *Embracing the Call to Spiritual Depth: Gifts for Contemplative Living.* New York: Paulist, 2010.

Harding, M. Esther. *Woman's Mysteries, Ancient and Modern.* Boston: Shambhala, 1990.

Hess, Lisa M. *Artisanal Theology: Intentional Formation in Radically Covenantal Companionship.* Eugene, OR: Cascade, 2009.

———. "Toward an *Intimacy of Difference*: Philosophical and Theological Resources for Human Connection through Difference." In *Alienation and Connection: Suffering in a Global Era*, edited by Lisa Withrow, 97–114. Lanham, MD: Lexington, 2011.

Isherwood, Lisa. *The Power of Erotic Celibacy: Queering Heterosexuality.* Queering Theology. New York: T. & T. Clark, 2006.

Johnson, Mark. *Moral Imagination: Implications of Cognitive Science for Ethics.* Chicago: University of Chicago Press, 1993.

Kepnes, Steven. *Jewish Liturgical Reasoning.* New York: Oxford University Press, 2003.

Kidd, Sue Monk, and Ann Kidd Taylor. *Traveling with Pomegranates: A Mother-Daughter Story.* New York: Viking, 2009.

Kula, Irwin, with Linda Loewenthal. *Yearnings: Embracing the Sacred Messiness of Life.* New York: Hyperion, 2006.

Largen, Kristin Johnston, with Mary E. Hess and Christy Lohr Sapp. *Interreligious Learning and Teaching: A Christian Rationale for Transformative Praxis.* Seminarium Elements. Minneapolis: Fortress, 2014.

Lewis, C. S. *Surprised by Joy.* New York: Harcourt Brace Jovanovich, 1966.

Marion, Jean-Luc. *The Erotic Phenomenon.* Translated by Stephen E. Lewis. Chicago: University of Chicago Press, 2007.

———. *God Without Being: Hors-texte.* Translated by Thomas A. Carlson. Chicago: University of Chicago Press, 1991.

May, Gerald. "From Cruelty to Compassion: The Crucible of Personal Transformation." http://fetzer.org/sites/default/files/images/resources/attachment/2012-07-12/dad_may_essay.pdf.

Oliver, Mary Anne McPherson. *Conjugal Spirituality: The Primacy of Mutual Love in Christian Tradition.* Kansas City: Sheed & Ward, 1994.

Olthuis, James H., ed. "Crossing the Threshold: Sojourning Together in the Wild Spaces of Love." In *Knowing Other-Wise: Philosophy at the Threshold of Spirituality*, edited by James H. Olthuis, 235–53. New York: Fordham University Press, 1997.

———. "Introduction: Love/Knowledge; Sojourning with Others, Meeting with Differences." In *Knowing Other-Wise: Philosophy at the Threshold of Spirituality*, edited by James H. Olthuis, 1–15. New York: Fordham University Press, 1997.

Ong, Walter J. *Orality and Literacy: The Technologizing of the Word.* New York: Routledge, 1982, 2002.

Palmer, Parker. "Thirteen Ways of Looking at Community . . . with a Fourteenth Thrown in for Free." July 10, 2014. http://www.couragerenewal.org/13-ways-of-looking-at-community_parker-palmer/.

Rimon, Yosef Zvi. "Kiddush—Parts 1–3." *Israel Koschitzky Virtual Beit Midrash.* Translated by David Silverberg. www.haretzion.org.

Rollins, Peter. *The Fidelity of Betrayal: Towards a Church beyond Belief.* Brewster, MA: Paraclete, 2008.

Ross, Maggie. *Silence: A User's Guide*, vol. 1, *Process*. Eugene, OR: Cascade, 2014.

———. *Writing the Icon of the Heart: In Silence Beholding.* Eugene, OR: Cascade, 2013.

BIBLIOGRAPHY

Schnarch, David. *Passionate Marriage: Keeping Love and Intimacy Alive in Committed Relationships*. New York: Norton, 2009.

Schneiders, Sandra M. "Approaches to the Study of Christian Spirituality." In *The Blackwell Companion to Christian Spirituality*, edited by Arthur Holder, 15–33. Malden, MA: Blackwell, 2005.

Schreiber, Doniel. "*Kiddush*: A Halakhic Overview—Part I." *Alei Etzion* 8 (1999) 71–84. www.etzion.org.il/vbm/english/alei/8-7newds-kiddush.rtf.

Stafford, William. *Stories That Could Be True: New and Collected Poems*. New York: Harper & Row, 1977.

Steinsaltz, Adin. "An Additional Note on the *Kiddush* Ritual." In *The Thirteen Petalled Rose: A Discourse on the Essence of Jewish Existence and Belief*, translated by Yehuda Hanegbi, 153–58. New York: Basic Books, 2006.

———. *Opening the Tanya: Discovering the Moral and Mystical Teachings of a Classic Work of Kabbalah*. Hebrew text edited by Meir Hanegbi. Translated by Yaacov Tauber. San Francisco: Jossey-Bass, 2003.

Taylor, Barbara Brown. *Leaving Church: A Memoir of Faith*. New York: HarperOne, 2012.

Ullman, Robert, and Judyth Reichenberg-Ullman. *Mystics, Masters, Saints, and Sages: Stories of Enlightenment*. Berkeley: Conari, 2001.

Washburn, Michael. *Embodied Spirituality in a Sacred World*. Albany: State University of New York Press, 2003.

Welwood, John. *Journey of the Heart: The Path of Conscious Love*. New York: Harper, 1990.

Whitman, Walt. *Leaves of Grass: The First (1855) Edition*. New York: Penguin, 1959.

Zalman, Shneur. *Tanya, the Masterpiece of Hasidic Wisdom: Selections Annotated and Explained*. Translation and annotation by Rami Shapiro. Woodstock, VT: SkyLight Paths, 2010.

www.ingramcontent.com/pod-product-compliance
Lightning Source LLC
Chambersburg PA
CBHW020853160426
43192CB00007B/907